THE BRITISH MP

To my parents

The British MP

A socio-economic study of the House of Commons

COLIN MELLORS

SAXON HOUSE

Published by
Saxon House, Teakfield Limited,
Westmead, Farnborough, Hants., England

ISBN 0 566 00138 1

Printed in Great Britain by Biddles Limited, Guildford, Surrey.
Typeset by Supreme Litho Typesetting, Goodmayes, Ilford, Essex.

Contents

Acknowledgements

The publication of a book is an opportunity to express debts and gratitudes which are frequently neglected. It is a pleasure, therefore, to take this opportunity of thanking a few friends and colleagues who have generously encouraged, advised and criticised.

I am indebted to Professor Hugh Berrington who not only encouraged me to publish the original research upon which this book is based, but also offered advice in its preparation. Equally grateful thanks are owed to Stuart Walkland who guided this research. To John Irwin, of Saxon House, I must express my thanks for much useful advice and considerable patience. If I can be allowed a final indulgence, I am grateful to W. Thornhill and K.W. Watkins, of Sheffield University, not for any advice in the preparation of this book, but for helping stimulate my interest in the study of politics.

Needless to say, any misinterpretations are my own doing.

Colin Mellors
September 1977

1 The study of political recruitment

'. . . political machinery does not act of itself. As it is first made, so it has to be worked by men, and even by ordinary men. It needs not their simple acquiescence, but their active participation, and must be adjusted to the capacities and qualities of such men as are available.'

J.S. Mill

The notion of representative government is central to the British political system and, to a large extent, the quality of such government is determined by the individuals who collectively constitute Parliament. Moreover, in a representative democracy the major political power of the electorate lies in its ability to choose who shall rule. Members of Parliament are thus key figures in the process of government in Britain. Although much energy has been devoted to describing and evaluating Members' roles and activities inside and, to some extent, outside Parliament, rather less systematic attention has been paid to the nature of political recruitment in Britain. Material about the backgrounds of MPs tends to be scattered, occasionally conflicting and at best episodic. This study consequently remedies this situation by examining in some detail the changing socio-economic profile of British MPs during the period 1945–1974.

The purpose of this study is two-fold. By collecting and analysing standard socio-economic background data on all the 1,758 Members who have successfully contested one or more of the ten post-war general elections, it is hoped to produce a clearer and more accurate picture of the changing pattern of recruitment to the British House of Commons during the past thirty years. As such it may act as a source of reference.

However, if the study of political recruitment is to be more than an entertaining exercise in social arithmetic, it is necessary to consider the significance of the features which this kind of analysis produces. That the British House of Commons is, like legislatures throughout the world, socially untypical is hardly surprising. Territorial, as opposed to interest representation is unlikely ever to produce a set of representatives who are a social microcosm of society. But the ways in which the legislature does exclude some social groups and, more particularly, the manner in which political recruitment has changed since 1945 may well have considerable implications not only for the character of political decisions but also for the strength and nature of ideological groups within Parliament. The last chapter of this book, therefore, concentrates upon the political, parliamentary and ideological implications of the rapidly changing socio-economic composition of the post-war British House of Commons.

Recruitment studies

The use of recruitment studies as a tool of political analysis has spread extensively since the early 1950s [1]. Besides providing a greater understanding of individual political systems and institutions, it has come to be an important feature in the comparative study of political systems and over these twenty or so years, this general line of inquiry has separated into three specialisms.

The first has concentrated upon the identification, differentiation and operation of particular select and influential groupings in society [2]. These are the élite studies whose primary concern is the location of power. A second, but less well-researched, specialism has attempted to throw light upon the factors which cause some individuals to seek public office. Using mainly methods of psychological enquiry, it focuses attention on the motivations, attitudes and ambitions of those involved in various levels of public office. Whilst potentially the most illuminating in explaining which factors differentiate the active from passive in politics, this branch of recruitment studies has probably been least satisfactory and, methodologically, most problematic. The third specialism, and the approach which is adopted here, is to select a defined élite and examine in some detail, the more important biographic and career data about the members of this élite group. For convenience, and also as a result of prior assumptions about the location of power, such studies generally concentrate upon the holders of public office [3].

A prime purpose of this latter approach is fashioned by one interpretation of the word 'representative' − the extent to which political élites reflect the social composition of the mass population [4]. Indeed for some early studies, the degree to which the social composition of the national legislature matches the electorate as a whole appears as a vital test of representative government in a liberal democracy [5]. One important study of American senators lists throughout its analysis of politicians' backgrounds, an index of over-representation [6]. But élite/mass comparisons carry design problems and have limited usefulness. As such, they have been avoided in this study of post-war British MPs. Much more important are the shifting configurations of the élite group since they indicate changing opportunities for élite access. In terms of British parliamentary recruitment, this is most clearly seen by the rapid displacement of manual workers by members of professional groups in the Parliamentary Labour Party (PLP) during the post-war period. On the evidence of other research, biographic data may also be indicative of the nature of ideological groupings and, to a lesser degree, attitudes assumed by those in public office. But this secondary concern has been less rigorously researched.

As the popularity of recruitment studies has grown, so has the intensity of its critics. Much of this criticism is directed at the rather ambitious aspirations of some of the early recruitment studies and may be explained by a frequent failure to appreciate the precise aims and context of the social background approach. It is a short step from arguing that the social profile of our political leaders is an important way of understanding the opportunities available for political recruitment to suggesting that a set of socio-economic background variables are the main causal factor in the attitudes and preferences adopted by these leaders.

The aspirations of some early studies can be illustrated by an extract from the introduction of an otherwise excellent and pioneering study of American senators.

> Who are the United States senators? How did they get there? Why do some men become senators while others do not? Do a senator's personal background and pre-Senate experiences make any difference to how he behaves in office? How do senators define their role? What are their patterns of work? ... Who is influential and why? ... why do senators vote the way they do? How do they make up their minds? The list could be greatly extended ... [7]

No doubt it could, but clearly one volume of research is likely to be able to provide little more than a vague insight into a few of these questions. Equally problematic are the less specific, but wider, ambitions. The same scholar else-where suggests, not unreasonably, that:

> the study of the social backgrounds of political decision-makers ... contributes to a deeper understanding of the actions and decisions of those in positions of authority [8].

If this is intended to imply that attitudes are affected by social experiences, then it is not a statement with which social psychologists would find difficulty in concurring. If, however, it is intended to imply some specific and quantifiable relationship between biographic data and political attitudes, it becomes more speculative and difficult to substantiate. It is a simple matter to observe how some British politicians can have very similar social backgrounds and yet adopt ideological positions at the opposite extremes of their political party. For those who prefer a more systematic denunciation of background/attitudinal congruence, the last decade has seen the publication of much persuasive evidence [9]. One result of this research is to suggest the need for further study into the second specialism of recruitment studies — the studies of motivation and attitude [10].

The social background approach has been especially questioned about two aspects of its conventional design. First, as Edinger and Searing have suggested, there has been a general failure to substantiate the notion that knowledge about a person's social origins will, of itself, be predictive of later attitudes and preferences. They argue that political rather than social background is a stronger predictor of preferences. A second concern, which follows from this, is the reliance in this 'harmless form of voyeurism ... on Tired Old Variables' [11]. It is a valid point which goes right to the crux of this kind of approach because quite simply we can only consider the measurable and the obtainable. It is obviously much easier to investigate objective attributes rather than opinions, attitudes and experiences which are almost impossible to discover let alone measure. This was recognised in the 1970 Nuffield Election Study.

We have learnt to be suspicious of building too heavy a superstructure of conclusions on such necessarily shaky foundations . . . there is a temptation to be too much influenced by characteristics which readily lend themselves to measurement. Intelligence, humanity and emotional stability are much less easily discoverable than education, age and occupation [12].

The publication of another recruitment study is therefore an excellent opportunity to clarify the objectives of analysing social backgrounds. On the question of background/attitude relationships, no specific and causal relationships between social background and issue preferences are suggested or even assumed. Conversely, it should be pointed out that recent studies of factors affecting issue preference have argued against simple correlations between social background and attitudes but not denied that social experience had any relevance for the framework in which political preferences are selected or for the tastes and life styles of those who practise politics. It is important, therefore, to point to other research which has attempted to trace, in a systematic manner, the consequences of the social attributes of MPs relative to the nature of the decisions which they take. By analysing signatories to Early Day Motions (EDMs) Hugh Berrington has been able to show some important correlations between certain attributes and political attitudes as expressed in them [13]. The use of EDMs as an expression of attitude does, of course, have the advantage that, in contrast to actual voting records, they are less affected by the constraints of party whips and constituency party pressures. Thus while it is not suggested that socio-economic factors are the main determinants of opinion or preference, some social attributes do give greater force to intra-party, if not inter-party, cleavages.

A further contribution of the conventional social background approach is its usefulness as an indicator of party cohesion. The essential homogeneity and common social origins of the Conservative Party stands in sharp contrast to the more heterogeneous nature of the Parliamentary Labour Party. While similarities do not necessarily determine political preferences, their impact on intra-party cohesion and cooperation seems much more plausible. The diverse nature of the Labour Party in Parliament clearly serves to exacerbate existing tensions and conflicts within that party — although this should not be taken to imply that the Conservative Party is without internal conflict [14].

As a symbolic factor, social attributes have an importance in British politics. In Labour circles especially, social origins have an important value in themselves, irrespective of the political attitudes which they may or may not influence. A decline in numbers of working class representatives is, for many Labour supporters, itself a highly unsatisfactory process and, given the class basis of much of British voting preferences, it signals an accelerating incongruence between the background of Labour supporters and voters and their representatives in Parliament [15].

This leads to perhaps the most important single justification for continuing and refining social background approaches, namely the light which they throw onto the opportunities for political recruitment. This can be especially valuable where

4

the technique of cohort analysis is applied and changes over time are measured. Such a technique is applied here and, besides 'cameos' of successive Parliaments, there is a record of the successive cohorts of new and departing MPs. For these reasons the analysis of legislative recruitment through the study of social background still has considerable value for the better understanding of a political system; incomplete findings remain better than none.

Scope of study

Interest in the social and economic backgrounds of MPs can be traced back to H.J. Laski and one of the first surveys was by one of his students, J.A. Thomas, covering the period 1832–1901 [16]. J.F.S. Ross, in his *Parliamentary Representation*, covered the period 1918–35 in greater detail and, using a refined method of analysis, extended this to 1955 in his *Elections and Electors* [17]. Since 1945, the *Nuffield Election Studies* have included data on the socio-economic composition of successive Parliaments [18]. P.W. Buck has looked from a particular, and somewhat narrow viewpoint at the Members elected between 1918 and 1959 [19], and, of course, Guttsman's *The British Political Elite* (recently up-dated in an article by R.W. Johnson) throws considerable light on the wider political élite [20]. Andrew Roth's excursions into the business backgrounds of MPs are a continual mine of information and entertainment [21]. There have been two major studies of British candidate selection in recent years [22] and the last few years have seen the publication of a number of studies in the field of élites and élite recruitment [23]. Despite this apparent plethora of recruitment studies an essential problem is that there has been no work which fully covers the period as a whole as well as analysing the changing configurations of recruitment opportunities longitudinally through successive elections. Moreover, the employment of varying methodologies makes inferences from a combination of works a somewhat suspect exercise and it is in this capacity that the present study is intended as a source of reference on British parliamentary recruitment [24].

The year 1945 was clearly a watershed in political and electoral history. The previous election had, because of the suspension of normal electoral arrangements during the Second World War, been held some ten years earlier and a consequence of this was the mass intake of new faces following the election of July 1945. Of the 640 MPs elected, 327 had never sat in the House before. For statistical comparisons, the period is also useful since no party dominated these ten elections of which, in contrast to their pre-war fortunes, Labour won six and the Conservatives four. The Conservatives held office for seventeen of these thirty years and Labour the remaining thirteen years. The ten elections saw the election of some 815 Conservative Members and 860 Labour Members. There is clearly reasonable balance between the parties, which is helpful in making statistical comparisons.

Reference has already been made to the difficulty of accurately combining and comparing the results of different surveys. No two studies present similar information in an identical manner and there is often a real dispute about the reliability of data in the first place. Data requires collection, collation and interpretation – all with a measure of consistency and in this context, consistency is probably more relevant than any attempt to present an absolute and definitive picture. Therefore, the same sources have been called upon throughout, a uniform methodology has been employed and, since the period is studied as a whole any inferences from the data even if subjective and tentative, should at least be consistent.

A frequent concern of those who have considered the social composition of political élites is a comparison with the social profile of the electorate and inevitably the findings of such a comparison is that the élite is grossly untypical of society. Quite simply, random samples never appear in these circumstances and 'microcosmic' representation is only ever likely to emerge if 'the House of Commons comes to be composed of conscripts chosen by computer' [25]. As one political columnist has rightly observed,

> We are still in thrall to the 19th century liberal fallacy that political involvement is good for you, therefore everyone should do it. We ought to recognise that political activity is a minority, even an eccentric, taste [26].

History is not without those who have indeed argued strongly against a legislature which is typical of those whom they represent.

> It is said to be necessary, that all classes of citizens should have some of their own number in the representative body, in order that their feelings and interests may be the better understood and attended to. But we have seen that this will never happen under any arrangement that leaves the votes of the people free. Where this is the case, the representative body, with too few exceptions to have any influence on the spirit of the government, will be composed of landholders, merchants, and men of the learned professions. But where is the danger that the interests and feelings of the different classes of citizens will not be understood or attended to by these three descriptions of men? [27]

As such, the desirability or otherwise of any legislature reflecting the social composition of society is ignored here. However, there are two refinements to this élite-society comparison which are worthy of consideration. If the word 'society' is replaced by the word 'voters', the comparison is more meaningful. Similarly, although we may not be concerned with the nuances of the opportunity structure for political recruitment, where changing patterns of recruitment so radically shift as to almost completely displace one previously fundamental section, important political consequences must ensue. We may add, therefore, these concerns to our rationale in studying political recruitment.

Standard biographic attributes are well established in social background studies. They generally include such variables as age, education, occupation, local political experience, and previous electoral contests. Similar variables are examined here and generally related to the main variables of party. In addition two particular sub-groups — women and sponsored MPs — are examined separately. In general, the approach is to examine party by one variable by cohort rather than party by one variable (say, education) by another variable (say, occupation). The usefulness of the latter technique is that one attribute often reinforces another in a measurable way (e.g. Labour elementary educated, sponsored; manual workers), but this has been sacrificed, in terms of aggregate data at least, in favour of an emphasis on change over time.

In the absence of any specific and widely acceptable tools to determine the effect of social background on later attitudes and policy preferences, perhaps the most useful analysis of recruitment is to be found by the examination of individual variables longitudinally [28]. Quite simply, this means to focus attention on change in social profile over, in this case, ten distinct points of time. This is probably most effectively portrayed by using cohort analysis to examine incremental change over time, separating the group of new MPs entering at any election. Incremental change, as displayed by the cohorts of new MPs has the particular advantage over simply showing ten 'cameos' of the total composition of the House, in that they are not time-lagged. The effect on overall composition is delayed by the effect of political longevity and the existence of so large a proportion of 'safe' seats in the British House of Commons.

Methodology

The most important feature of the methodology used here is the distinction which is made between three types of MP — *all*, *new* and *departing*. Most studies of British parliamentary recruitment have contented themselves with descriptions of the social composition of Parliament at any given election and not attempted to distinguish between the characteristics of those arriving at, and those leaving, Westminster. *New* refers to those Members winning their first general election and *departing* to those winning their last general election in this period. Consequently, the new MPs of, say, February 1974 replaced the departing MPs of 1970 (i.e. those whose last general election victory was in 1970) [29]. The basic criterion for inclusion is victory at a general election. Therefore Members whose successes have been limited to by-election victories are excluded from this study. An incidental consequence of this is that a Member may, in fact, have already been in Parliament for a few years as a result of a by-election success before his first recording as new here [30]. Apart from this slight complication, the use of this twin approach is designed to stress the changing characteristics of parliamentary recruitment over these ten elections. As a rule, the data on *all* and *new* MPs is contained in the body of the book and *departing* MPs are recorded in the appendix. Particular attention has been paid to the cohorts of new MPs in a party when that party loses the general election, because clearly any new MPs who are elected at a time when their party is faring badly nationally must be contesting the 'safer' seats and as such, they are perhaps the strongest clues to the changing recruitment preferences of the political parties.

Traditional sources of background information have been used [31]. In contrast with some European countries, official data about Members of Parliament is almost non-existent and the guarded nature of some MPs was well illustrated by the attitude of some towards the recent establishment of a register of MPs' interests [32]. Despite the difficulties, however, the overall rate of missing data (shown as INA in the tables) is small (Table 1.1). In the case of age, as would be expected, most of the missing data is explained by the customary discretion of women in these matters. If no information was available about a Member's experience in local government or previous electoral contests, then it is assumed he had none. Where percentages are shown, they refer to Members upon whom information is available.

Table 1.1
Information not available (percentages)

	Age	Education	Occupation
Conservative	1·6	2·3	1·0
Labour	3·6	1·6	1·5
Other	3·6	6·0	1·2
Total	2·7	2·2	1·3

The aggregate data itself should appear fairly self-explanatory. It should be noted here, however, that the approach when searching for occupational and educational data was largely guided by a desire to record formative, though not necessarily first, backgrounds. When a person becomes a Member of Parliament he will generally assume the status which public affairs ascribe and recruitment studies have naturally focused on social origins and previous experiences. For those who suggest correlations of background and attitudes, formative data is, by definition, paramount. Equally for those whose concern is with the opportunity structure for advancement into the political élite, this same priority is appropriate. Although the choice of formative backgrounds is obviously a matter of judgment in the case of multiple occupations and educations, the statistical implication of this approach is that only one occupational and one educational background is recorded for each MP.

The study of legislative recruitment through the analysis of social backgrounds retains much value in facilitating the better understanding of representative government. Social and economic backgrounds cannot, of course, be isolated from other political and psychological factors in the formation of political attitudes, but nevertheless must have effect upon the nature of these attitudes. Social cleavages serve to exacerbate existing ideological and attitudinal divisions. As a symbolic factor, social identity makes a contribution to the conduct of politics and, most obvious of all, it tells us something about the changing opportunities for access to public office. If, as Ronald Butt suggests, Parliament 'cannot easily rise above the contemporary political climate' [33] , then neither can it rise above the personnel of Parliament.

Notes

[1] For early use and discussion of the concept see, L.G. Seligman, 'Recruitment in Politics', *Political Research Organisation and Design*, 1958 and his study of leadership in Oregon, *Western Political Quarterly*, 1959. Donald R. Matthews', *The Social Background of Political Decision Makers*, Doubleday, 1954, is, of course, a pioneering work in this field. For a useful review of the development of recruitment studies, see D.V. Fleischer, *Thirty Years of Legislative Recruitment in Brazil* (a paper presented to the Tenth World Congress of the International Political Science Association, 1976) pp. 4–11 and his extensive bibliography.

[2] See G. Parry, *Political Elites*, Allen and Unwin, London, 1969 and T.B. Bottomore, *Elites and Society*, Watts, London, 1964. The most distinguished study of British political leaders is, of course, W.L. Guttsman, *The British Political Elite*, MacGibbon and Kee, London, 1964.

[3] A bibliography of recruitment studies in varied areas – political, administrative, economic, military, the church, judiciary, educational, trade union and local – is contained in I. Crewe (ed.), *British Political Sociology Yearbook: Elites in Western Democracy*, Croom Helm, London, 1974, pp. 337–350.

[4] For a discussion of the concept of representation, see A.H. Birch, *Representation*, Macmillan, London, 1971.

[5] See J.F.S. Ross, *Elections and Electors*, Eyre and Spottiswoode, London, 1955, and his earlier *Parliamentary Representation*, Eyre and Spottiswoode, London, 1948.

[6] Donald R. Matthews, *U.S. Senators and Their World*, Vintage Books, New York, 1960. The ratio (% of senators possessing attributes 'A')÷(% of population possessing attribute 'A') is given to be the index of representation. 'An index smaller than 1·0 means that the attribute is under-represented; an index of 1·0 means perfect representation; an index of 2·0 indicates twice the expected proportion and so on', pp. 273–4. However, Matthews does make clear that he is using this term in a statistical sense and not 'imply that members of the Senate *ought* to be exactly like the people they represent' (p. 13). For reasons given this kind of detailed comparison of the social profiles of MPs and electors is not included here.

[7] Ibid., p. 8.

[8] Matthews, *The Social Background of Political Decision-Makers*, p. 4.

[9] See especially, L.J. Edinger and D. Searing, 'Social Background in Elite Analysis: A Methodological Inquiry', *American Political Science Review*, 1967; D. Searing,'The Comparative Study of Elite Socialisation', *Comparative*

Politics, vol. 1; D. Fairlie and I. Budge, 'Élite Background and Issue Preferences: A Comparison of British and Foreign Data using a New Technique', in Crewe op. cit., pp. 199–240.

[10] I. Budge and D. Fairlie, 'Political Recruitment and Dropout: Predictive Success of Background Characteristics over Five British Localities', *British Journal of Political Science*, vol. 5, pp. 33–68.

[11] Crewe, op. cit., pp. 20–4.

[12] D. Butler and M. Pinto-Duschinsky, *The British General Election of 1970*, Macmillan, London, 1971, p. 299.

[13] S.E. Finer, H.B. Berrington, D.J. Bartholomew, *Backbench Opinion in the House of Commons, 1955–59*, Pergamon, 1961; H.B. Berrington, *Backbench Opinion in the House of Commons, 1945–55*, Pergamon, London, 1973. I am grateful to Professor Berrington for letting me see early results of his study (with John Leece and Norman Squirrell) of backbench motions for the period 1959–76.

[14] See P. Seyd 'Factionalism within the Conservative Party', *Government and Opposition*, 1972.

[15] See, for example, B. Hindess, *The Decline of Working Class Politics*, MacGibbon and Kee, London, 1971.

[16] J.A. Thomas, *The House of Commons, 1832–1901: A Study of its Economic and Functional Character*, University of Wales Press, Cardiff, 1939.

[17] J.F.S. Ross, *Parliamentary Representation*, Eyre and Spottiswoode, London, 1948, and J.F.S. Ross, *Elections and Electors*, Eyre and Spottiswoode, London, 1955.

[18] R.B. McCallum and A. Readman, *The British General Election of 1945*
H.G. Nicholas, *The British General Election of 1950*
D.E. Butler, *The British General Election of 1951*
D.E. Butler, *The British General Election of 1955*
D.E. Butler and R. Rose, *The British General Election of 1959*
D.E. Butler and A. King, *The British General Election of 1964*
D.E. Butler and A. King, *The British General Election of 1966*
D.E. Butler and M. Pinto-Duschinsky, *The British General Election of 1970*
D.E. Butler and D. Kavanagh, *The British General Election of February 1974*
D.E. Butler and D. Kavanagh, *The British General Election of October 1974*
(All published by Macmillan)

[19] P.W. Buck, *Amateurs and Professionals in British Politics 1918–59*, University of Chicago Press, Chicago, 1963.

[20] W. L. Guttsman, *The British Political Elite*, MacGibbon and Kee, London, 1963, and R.W. Johnson, *The British Political Elite, 1955–70*, European Journal of Sociology, 1973.

[21] A. Roth and J. Kerbey, *The Business Background of MPs*, Parliamentary Profile Services, London, 1972. (See also 1963, 1965 and 1967 editions.)

[22] A. Ranney, *Pathways to Parliament*, University of Wisconsin, Madison, 1965; M.D. Rush, *The Selection of Parliamentary Candidates*, Nelson, London, 1969.

[23] See, for example, I. Crewe (ed.) op. cit.; P. Stanworth and A. Giddons (ed.) *Elites and Power in British Society*, Cambridge University Press, London, 1974; J. Urry and J. Wakeford (eds) *Power in Britain*, Heinemann Educational, London, 1973.

[24] This point can be seen if an attempt is made to discover the number of public school men in the 1970 Parliament. *The Times House of Commons* suggests the figure to be 191. In just one table, the Nuffield Study calculates this to be both 296 and 310. Finally, according to calculations made for this study, which are in part based upon individual entries in The Times' guides, the figure should be 304.

	Times	*Nuffield*	*This study*
Conservative	166	247 (or 243)	243
Labour	22	60 (or 50)	56
Other	3	3 (3)	3
	191	310 (or 296)	304

[25] A.H. Birch, 'The Theory of Representation and Practice' in S.E. Finer (ed.) *Adversary Politics and Electoral Reform*, Anthony Wigram, London, 1975, p. 57.

[26] Alan Watkins, 'The Rejection of Party', *New Statesman*, 1.11.73.

[27] Alexander Hamilton, *The Federalist*, No. 35. See also S. Krislov, *Representative Bureaucracy*, Prentice-Hall, 1974, p. 15, for the distinction between representational and functional representation.

[28] This appears to be one of the few common areas of agreement between students of the social background approach and their critics: see Fleischer, op. cit., p. 47; Guttsman's essay in Stanworth and Giddons (eds) op. cit., p. 26; Crewe (ed.) op. cit., p. 25. This paragraph leans heavily on Fleischer's explanation of his approach in studying Brazilian legislative recruitment.

[29] The *departing* MPs at one election do not numerically equal the *new* arrivals at the next election since MPs may have breaks in their parliamentary careers and return at a subsequent election. Such Members are not classified as *departing* until they finally leave Parliament (or, at least, had not returned by October 1974). Clearly, some of the February 1974 departures may return to the Commons at a future date outside the time-span of this study. It should also be noted here that a number of MPs have crossed the Floor of the House and have been returned at a subsequent election as a member of a different party. Party labels are attached in the tables appropriately. Hence a man may be *new* under one party and *departing* under another. Fortunately, transfers were fairly rare until 1974 when Enoch Powell and the Ulster Unionists changed their classifications from 'Conservative' to 'Other'.

[30] For example, K. Baker (Conservative) is not here recorded as *new* until February 1974 even though he had by then been in Parliament nearly 6 years. He won a by-election in 1968, but then did not win the 1970 General

Election. He found himself in Parliament later in 1970 as a result of a second by-election victory, but had to wait until February 1974 for his first general election victory.

[31] These are: *Dod's Parliamentary Companion*; successive *Times Guides to the House of Commons; Who's Who; Who was Who*; successive editions of *Labour's Election Who's Who*; Roth op. cit.

[32] The difficulties of gathering useful data is illustrated by the entries on two MPs in the Time Guide in the early part of this period. Despite severe restrictions on available column inches, the entries have some information which is hardly helpful to the social science researcher: R. Boothby (*Times Guide, 1955*) 'A Champion of the virtues of herring as food'. E. Graham Little (*Times Guide, 1945*) '. . . distinguished medical specialist, who during the war has specially interested himself in the quality of the national loaf'.

[33] R. Butt, *The Power of Parliament*, (2nd ed.), Constable, London, 1969, p. 159.

2 Pathways to Westminster

Partisanship and general elections

Even the briefest glance at the 1,758 Members who have been elected in this period reveals that first and foremost a party ticket is a necessary prerequisite of electoral success. Membership of a political party, usually one or other of the two major parties, has been the most common characteristic of post-war British MPs. Less than 5 per cent of all Members successfully contesting the ten general elections in this period did so without the support of either the Conservative or Labour parties.

Of the 1,758 Members, 815 were elected as representatives of the Conservative Party and 860 as representatives of the Labour Party. Included in the former group are those Ulster Unionists who were elected for Northern Ireland Constituencies up to, and including, the 1970 General Election. Only 83 other Members were elected during this period and even this figure includes a handful of Members who, although they were successful at the polls, never took their places at Westminster. Two Sinn Fein Members elected in 1955, for example, were prevented from taking their seats because they were serving ten year prison sentences at the time of their election and at least another three Ulster Members never actually sat in the Commons.

The group of *other* Members, in fact, comprises a number of distinct elements. At the beginning of the period it includes a few individuals who are described as Independents although even these were sometimes elected with the tacit support of one of the parties or in the default of its candidates. Generally, however, they were elected as individuals and not as representatives of a particular party or movement and perhaps the most notable of this group was A.P. Herbert. But even at their strongest they were few in number and with the abolition of the University vote in 1948, they effectively disappeared from the parliamentary scene.

There has been a second variety of independent. These were the MPs who defected from one of the major parties and yet managed to hold their constituency despite losing the support of their former party. Three recent examples of successful Labour defectors are S.O. Davies (Merthyr Tydfil), E. Milne (Blyth) and D. Taverne (Lincoln). Davies had been a Member since 1934, but was denied the Labour candidature in 1970 because he was then 83 years old. He stood under the banner of 'Independent Labour', defeated the official Labour candidate by nearly 7,500 votes, and held the seat until his death in 1972. Milne and Taverne also lost the backing of their constituency parties and stood against the official Labour candidates in February 1974. Both were successful, Milne as an 'Independent Labour' candidate and Taverne as a 'Campaign for Social Democracy' candidate.

However, their successes were short-lived and they were both subsequently defeated by the official Labour candidates in the October General Election. Others attempting to continue despite the withdrawal of support from their constituency party, for example, E. Griffiths (Labour, Sheffield, Brightside in October 1974), have met with little success. The well known suggestion that no individual candidate is worth more than two or three per cent of the constituency vote appears as valid as ever.

Throughout the period, the fortunes of the Liberal Party have remained reasonably steady. There have been the ever present fears of virtually complete electoral annihilation and the periodic promise of a Liberal revival, especially following the Orpington by-election success of 1962 and immediately prior to the first General Election of 1974. In the event, little really changed. Their presence at Westminster continued but, despite some quite impressive successes in individual constituencies and a much improved share of the national vote, the operation of our electoral system has continued to restrict the size of their Westminster group. Since 1945, their number in the Commons has fluctuated between six and thirteen.

The most recent, and perhaps most significant group now outside the two major parties are the Nationalists. At the last general election 11 Scottish National Party and 3 Plaid Cymru Members were elected and, unlike the Liberals, there is a clear indication that the next general election may well bring further gains. In Scotland especially, their continued good showing in polls and local elections combined with their second placing in many constituencies in October 1974 suggests a further improvement next time. They have the additional advantage over the Liberals of more committed voter identification [1], and obviously much depends upon the development of the devolution issue.

Immediately following the 1970 election it would have appeared quite justifiable to suggest that this predominantly two party pattern of parliamentary representation would continue. The two party hegemony looked as secure as ever. At that election the share of the poll obtained by the combined efforts of the Conservative and Labour parties was 89·5 per cent, almost exactly what it had been at the 1950 General Election. From 1951 to 1970 inclusive, only 20 minor party MPs were returned, but the elections of 1974 brought about a considerable improvement in the fortunes of the minor parties. In the two General Elections of 1974, the combined Conservative and Labour share of the vote fell to 75 per cent. In fact, the share of the electorate obtained by these two parties has steadily declined since 1950, due largely to reduced turnouts. The 1974 elections are different, in so far as the massive drop in the combined Conservative and Labour share of the vote on these occasions can be directly attributed to voters changing their allegiances from the major to the minor parties. Hence the increased Liberal and Nationalists votes and current speculation about the durability of our two party system [2].

The effect of this change in voting patterns on parliamentary representation is quite clear. One third of the minor party MPs who have won general elections in this period did so at one or other of the 1974 elections. At the same elections, and for the first time in this period, the combined total of Conservative and Labour seats fell below 600: but this itself is the vital point. In the four general elections held in the fifties, Conservatives and Labour together were winning 98 per cent of the seats with 95 per cent of the vote. In the February and October 1974 elections they together polled only 75 per cent of the vote, but still captured 94 per cent of the seats. This is a clear illustration of how our simple majority electoral system favours the major parties. The effect in terms of parliamentary seats of any drift from the Conservative and Labour parties is consequently modified by the operation of this electoral system. Naturally enough, this apparent distortion between votes cast and seats won has led to renewed demands for electoral reform [3].

Notwithstanding these voting changes, the fact remains that the Conservative and Labour parties continue to dominate the Westminster scene. Furthermore, despite their novel party labels, the new minor MPs do not differ greatly in their backgrounds from the more traditional Members. This is not to say that changes in the composition of electoral support have no place in this kind of study. It is instructive, for example, to compare the changing character of electoral support for the Labour Party with the changing composition of that party at Westminster. It is sufficient to say here, however, that, in terms of parliamentary seats, the prevalent characteristics of this thirty year period have been the overwhelming successes of the Conservative and Labour parties and relative exclusion of potential MPs from other parties or groups. The impact of any decline in electoral partisanship has not yet really made itself felt in parliamentary terms, except in so far as it produced a Labour Government in a minority situation in February 1974 and with a slender majority, since eroded, the following October. Any distinct changes in this basic two party domination of the British Parliament will depend more upon the possible reform of our electoral system than continuing changes in voting behaviour.

Turnover

The electoral fortunes of most MPs are due less to election by a deliberative public than to selection by a constituency party's selection committee [4]. The first, and most important battle, therefore, to be won by an aspiring MP is to convince such a selection committee that he is the right candidate to represent their party and their constituency. His fate thereafter will be directly determined by the fortunes of his party both in the constituency and nationally.

British voting behaviour is conventionally renowned for its twin attributes of homogeneity and stability — although rather greater volatility is now becoming more common. The effect of this is to make two-thirds of constituencies safe, in that any normal national shift of support between the two major parties will not be sufficient to disturb the party which has traditionally held that seat. This may not necessarily be true at by-elections, when voters probably feel much freer to switch support or abstain in order to voice their criticism of, or occasionally support for, a party and its policies without disturbing the overall position of the parties in Parliament. There were some remarkable examples of exaggerated swings from Labour to Conservative, with the consequent losses of normally impregnable Labour seats, in the by-elections of 1976—77. But, in general, selection in a safe constituency all but guarantees success at the following general election. It is the prize which candidates most seek. Equally, selection in a constituency which the opposing party regards as safe will, miracles or political scandals apart, almost inevitably lead to electoral defeat. People choose to fight the unwinnable constituencies either because they feel that the experience will impress a selection committee in their search for a more hopeful seat next time, or because they are loyal party members with no Parliamentary aspirations, but with motivations to show the party banner and keep the constituency party alive. Given the increasing competition for candidatures, however, the latter are probably not that common, though they may be found much more frequently in local government elections.

The turnover of MPs from one general election to another is determined by two factors — shifts in relative support for the parties (usually measured in terms of 'net swing' [5] and the continuing process of replacement due to the resignation, retirement or death of sitting Members.

Those most vulnerable to changes of voting are, of course, the candidates who are contesting reasonably marginal constituencies where, say, a swing of 5 per cent or less will be sufficient to cause the seat to change hands. Whilst the vast majority of seats are not marginal and post-war swings have been very small in comparison with many other Western countries, the result, in terms of seats changing hands, of small changes of opinion is greatly exaggerated by the operation of the present electoral system. Consequently, a larger turnover is to be expected whenever there is a change of the party in power, an occasion which is usually marked by a higher than average swing in voters' preferences.

The process of natural replacement is fairly straightforward. At any general election, a number of Members will need to be replaced due to resignations, retirements or deaths. Naturally, this figure is likely to vary according to the gap between elections. The maximum time between elections is five years and the 1945 and 1959 Parliaments have come closest to running their full terms. In most cases retirement or resignation has been a voluntary activity.. This is not to say that MPs' relationships with their constituencies have been invariably harmonious, rather that when it came to their re-adoption few serious conflicts have emerged. In one study of general elections between 1950 and 1964, only thirty-four cases were discovered in which any real attempt had been made to question re-adoption [6]. In the majority of cases, re-adoption has been an almost automatic procedure. Recently, however, re-adoption conflicts have become more common, or at least received more public attention. The cases of S.O. Davies, E. Milne, D. Taverne and E. Griffiths have already been mentioned. In 1970, Nigel Fisher, Conservative MP for Surbiton, faced similar problems and the case of Reg Prentice's struggle in Newham, North East became a *cause célèbre*. In July 1975, the Constituency Labour Party had approved a resolution requiring Mr Prentice to submit himself for re-selection should he wish to be nominated as the Labour candidate at the next election. Two years of moves and counter-moves culminated in October 1977 when the former Cabinet minister resigned from the Labour Party and applied to join the Conservative Party. Whilst re-adoption conflicts are now occasionally evident in both parties, it appears to be the case that moves to replace Labour sitting Members are most likely to be successful [7]. The incidence of such conflicts no doubt strengthens the case for a review of selection procedures and possibly the involvement of more people in the actual selection process.

It is understandable that the largest turnover of Members came at the beginning of this period. In 1945, some 327 Members (including 244 Labour and 74 Conservative), over half of the House, found themselves at Westminster for the first time. The parliamentary experience of many others was limited to one or two years before 1945. Some Labour MPs, for example, sat during the 1929–31 Parliament, but were not subsequently re-elected until the 1945 General Election. The long delay between the 1935 and 1945 elections, because of the Second World War, resulted in that Parliament containing a larger proportion of new Members than any other this century. One spectator described the Chamber as a 'chaos of anonymous faces' [8]. On other occasions, the rate of turnover has varied according to voting patterns and the normal process of replacement. The actual figures are shown in Table 2.1 [9]. The 'pre-1945' column refers to any Member who first entered Parliament before the General Election of that year.

Table 2.1
Turnover: *new* Members, 1945–70

Election	Pre-1945	1945	1950	1951	1955	1959	1964	1966	1970	Feb. 1974	Oct. 1974	Total
Cons.	(182)	74	102	36	78	104	64	13	92	62	8	815
Labour	(161)	244	62	15	26	42	106	72	64	46	22	860
Other	(21)	9	5	2	2	1	6	5	4	21	7	83
Total	(364)	327	169	53	106	147	176	90	160	129	37	1758

It is easy to see the influence of the two factors of swing and replacement in these figures. During the period, there have been four changes of power – 1951, 1964, 1970 and February 1974 – and these changes of Government have been the occasion for a high turnover in the House. In 1964, the Labour victory saw 176 new Members (including 106 Labour and 64 Conservative). In June 1970, the election of Mr Heath's Conservative Government was the occasion for the appearance of 160 new Members (including 92 Conservative and 64 Labour). The 1951 and February 1974 changes of Government were a little more complicated. In the former instance, the Conservatives had already in the election of the previous year made inroads into the huge Labour majority of 1945. All that was required in 1951 was that final push to complete the Conservative victory. Thus, taking the 1950 and 1951 elections together, some 222 new faces appeared (including 138 Conservative and 77 Labour). The 1974 changeover was similar, but this time Labour gained power with a minority of seats and needed another election eight months later in order to achieve a working majority. Taking those two elections together, there were some 166 new recruits (including 86 Labour and 70 Conservative).

It is worth commenting upon the turnover at one other election, the 1959 General Election. Although there was no change of Government on this occasion, the Conservatives simply consolidated their position, 147 new Members were elected that year. This was a case of accentuated replacement when a larger than normal number of MPs, especially on the Labour side, took the opportunity to retire from active political life. Many of these were prewar veterans.

Electoral experience

Once selected by a constituency party a prospective Member has to face the ballot box before he finds himself on the benches at Westminster. For those candidates nominated by a party which holds a safe seat this is, of course, largely a formality. But for many, election to Parliament only comes after a number of previous abortive attempts. Aggregate data on the electoral experience of successful candidates is shown in Table 2.2.

Table 2.2
Members contesting seats prior to first successful election

Conservative			Labour			Other			Total		
Contests	No. MPs	%	Contests	No. MPs	%	Contests	No. MPs	%	Contests	No. MPs	%
1	214	26·3	1	181	21·0	1	16	19·3	1	411	23·4
2	115	14·1	2	94	10·9	2	7	8·4	2	216	12·3
3	23	2·8	3	36	4·2	3	2	2·4	3	61	3·5
4	2	0·2	4	12	1·4	4	1	1·2	4	15	0·9
5+	1	0·1	5+	4	0·5	5+	2	2·4	5+	7	0·4
Nil	460	56.5	Nil	533	62·0	Nil	55	66·3	Nil	1048	59·5
Total	815	100·0	Total	860	100·0	Total	83	100·0	Total	1758	100·0

Of the 1,758 Members in this survey, 710 (40·5 per cent) were, in fact, defeated on one or more occasions before being elected to Parliament. Whilst the difference between the two major parties is slight, it might be suggested that, on the whole, Conservative candidates are less likely to find themselves being allocated a safe seat to contest at their first attempt to enter Parliament. Since 1945, 355 of the 815

Conservative Members (43·5 per cent) suffered defeat at the polls before their initial election to Parliament. This compares with the 327 out of 860 Labour MPs (38·0 per cent) who experienced electoral defeat prior to entering Parliament. The equivalent figure for minor party Members tends to be misleading: of these 83 Members, only 28 (33·7 per cent) had been previously defeated. This might appear to suggest that this group found it easiest to be elected. Clearly, however, any comparison with the Conservative and Labour figures would be unreal because of the great differences in their numerical strengths. Almost all the minor party candidates at any election are doomed to failure and they include not only the perpetual candidate who will continue his campaign through several unsuccessful elections but also the very many candidates who fight and lose, just once before retiring gracefully. Nevertheless, it would be true to say that the Nationalist MPs who were returned at the last two elections are the least electorally experienced of any group in Parliament. Although they differ little in their socio-economic profile from Members in the other parties, almost without exception they are new recruits to political life. An important contribution that has been made by the Scottish National Party (SNP) and Plaid Cymru (PLC) in recent years is that they have brought into politics a large group of participants who were not previously active in political life. It is a contribution which is sometimes overlooked. And at a time when the two major parties have been suffering a considerable and sustained decline in membership, it is that much more a remarkable achievement.

Of the two major parties, the Conservative Party appears to have less difficulty in recruitng suitable potential candidates. Consequently, Conservative Members are more likely to have fought unsuccessful campaigns prior to their first general election victory. Back in 1945 only 13·7 per cent of Conservatives returned at that election had suffered defeat on an earlier occasion: 86·3 per cent won their first parliamentary contest. In part this is explained by the fact that the ten year interval between the 1935 and 1945 elections had denied many the opportunity of seeking election to Westminster except at a by-election. This can be seen by comparing the successes of pre-1945 and 1945 new Members. Whilst 20·8 per cent of Conservatives elected for the first time before 1945 had been previously defeated, only 1·4 per cent of new Members in 1945 (just one person) had not entered Parliament at their first attempt (Table 2.5). In subsequent elections, the incidence of initial success has declined (Table 2.3). By 1970, for the first time more than half of all Conservative Members (53·4 per cent) had tasted electoral defeat prior to their first successful contest and this proportion had risen to 63·9 per cent by October 1974. Politicians may not always enjoy great public approval — criticism is an inevitable result of taking unpopular decisions and perhaps failing to meet rising public expectations — but, in the Conservative Party at least, there seems to be no shortage of candidates seeking election.

Of those who were unsuccessful at their first attempt, the majority were elected at their next contest. On the occasion of their second parliamentary contest 26·3 per cent of Conservative Members succeeded and 14·1 per cent were returned at their third attempt (Table 2.2). The number fighting more than two contests before

Table 2.3
Members contesting seats prior to first election (percentages)

(a) Conservative

Type of Member	Pre-1945	1945	1950	1951	1955	1959	1964	1966	1970	Feb. 1974	Oct. 1974
All	–	13·7	23·9	29·5	39·2	46·2	46·1	47·5	53·4	60·3	63·9
New	20·8	1·4	41·2	66·6	65·4	51·9	43·6	53·9	64·2	72·6	75·0
Departing	–	15·5	8·3	21·5	26·5	38·3	46·4	37·9	43·2	42·4	–

(b) Labour

Type of Member	Pre-1945	1945	1950	1951	1955	1959	1964	1966	1970	Feb. 1974	Oct. 1974
All	–	23·0	23·5	23·9	26·0	29·1	38·8	45·3	46·6	48·2	52·9
New	24·9	21·3	25·8	26·7	42·3	33·4	56·5	69·4	57·8	52·2	86·4
Departing	–	23·5	16·2	24·4	20·9	21·4	40·0	47·8	42·8	46·4	–

Table 2.4
All Members contesting seats before first election

Election date	Conservative Total MPs	Conservative Contests	Conservative No. MPs	Conservative %	Labour Total MPs	Labour Contests	Labour No. MPs	Labour %	Other Total MPs	Other Contests	Other No. MPs
1945	213	1	24	11·3	400	1	46	11·5	27	1	1
		2	4	1·9		2	29	7·2		2	1
		3	1	0·5		3	10	2·5		3	1
		4	–	–		4	5	1·3		4	1
		5	–	–		5	2	0·5		5	–
		Nil	183	86·3		Nil	308	77·0		Nil	23
		Total	213	100·0		Total	400	100·0		Total	27
1950	297	1	56	18·8	315	1	42	13·3	13	1	–
		2	13	4·4		2	23	·7·3		2	1
		3	2	0·7		3	5	1·6		3	–
		4	–	–		4	3	1·0		4	–
		5	–	–		5	1	0·3		5	–
		Nil	226	76·1		Nil	241	76·5		Nil	12
		Total	297	100·0		Total	315	100·0		Total	13
1951	320	1	72	22·6	295	1	41	13·8	10	1	1
		2	18	5·6		2	20	6·8		2	1
		3	4	1·3		3	6	2·0		3	–
		4	–	–		4	3	1·0		4	–
		5	–	–		5	1	0·3		5	–
		Nil	226	70·5		Nil	224	76·1		Nil	8
		Total	320	100·0		Total	295	100·0		Total	10

(Table continued on facing page)

Table 2.4 (continued)

	Conservative				Labour				Other		
Election date	Total MPs	Contests	No. MPs	%	Total MPs	Contests	No. MPs	%	Total MPs	Contests	No. MPs
1955	343	1	81	25·7	277	1	42	15·2	10	1	1
		2	41	12·0		2	20	7·2		2	1
		3	10	2·9		3	7	2·5		3	–
		4	2	0·6		4	2	0·7		4	–
		5	–	–		5	1	0·4		5	–
		Nil	209	60·8		Nil	204	74·0		Nil	8
		Total	343	100·0		Total	277	100·0		Total	10
1959	365	1	99	27·2	258	1	43	16·7	7	1	2
		2	56	15·3		2	23	8·9		2	–
		3	11	3·2		3	6	2·3		3	–
		4	2	0·5		4	2	0·8		4	–
		5	–	–		5	1	0·4		5	–
		Nil	197	53·8		Nil	183	70·9		Nil	5
		Total	365	100·0		Total	258	100·0		Total	7
1964	301	1	84	27·9	320	1	69	21·5	9	1	2
		2	45	14·9		2	38	12·0		2	1
		3	9	3·0		3	10	3·1		3	1
		4	1	0·3		4	5	1·6		4	–
		5	–	–		5	2	0·6		5	–
		Nil	162	53·9		Nil	196	61·2		NIl	5
		Total	301	100·0		Total	320	100·0		Total	9
1966	253	1	68	26·9	365	1	95	26·1	12	1	6
		2	43	17·0		2	51	14·0		2	1
		3	8	3·2		3	14	3·8		3	1
		4	1	0·4		4	4	1·1		4	–
		5	–	–		5	1	0·3		5+	1
		Nil	133	52·5		Nil	200	54·7		Nil	3
		Total	253	100·0		Total	365	100·0		Total	12
1970	330	1	94	28·5	290	1	73	25·2	10	1	3
		2	64	19·4		2	40	13·8		2	1
		3	17	5·2		3	17	5·9		3	–
		4	–	–		4	4	1·4		4	–
		5	1	0·3		5	1	0·3		5	–
		Nil	154	46·6		Nil	155	53·4		Nil	6
		Total	330	100·0		Total	290	100·0		Total	10
Feb. 1974	297	1	102	34·3	301	1	82	27·6	37	1	13
		2	62	20·9		2	42	14·0		2	4
		3	14	4·7		3	15	5·0		3	–
		4	–	–		4	7	2·3		4	–
		5	1	0·4		5+	2	0·6		5	1
		Nil	118	39·7		Nil	153	50·8		Nil	19
		Total	297	100·0		Total	301	100·0		Total	37

(Table continued overleaf)

Table 2.4 (continued)

Election date	Conservative				Labour				Other		
	Total MPs	Con-tests	No. MPs	%	Total MPs	Con-tests	No. MPs	%	Total MPs	Con-tests	No. MPs
Oct. 1974	277	1	100	36·1	319	1	94	29·5	39	1	15
		2	61	22·0		2	48	15·0		2	4
		3	15	5·4		3	18	5·6		3	–
		4	–	–		4	7	2·2		4	–
		5	1	0·4		5	2	0·6		5+	2
		Nil	100	36·1		Nil	150	47·1		Nil	18
		Total	277	100·0		Total	319	100·0		Total	39

Table 2.5
New Members contesting seats before first election

Election date	Conservative				Labour				Other		
	Total MPs	Con-tests	No. MPs	%	Total MPs	Con-tests	No. MPs	%	Total MPs	Con-tests	No. MPs
Pre-1945	182	1	30	16·5	161	1	22	13·7	21	1	1
		2	7	3·8		2	10	6·2		2	1
		3	1	0·5		3	4	2·5		3	1
		4	–	–		4	3	1·9		4	1
		5	–	–		5	1	0·6		5	–
		Nil	144	79·2		Nil	121	75·1		Nil	17
		Total	182	100·0		Total	161	100·0		Total	21
1945	74	1	1	1·4	244	1	24	9·8	9	1	–
		2	–	–		2	19	7·8		2	–
		3	–	–		3	6	2·5		3	–
		4	–	–		4	2	0·8		4	–
		5	–	–		5	1	0·4		5	–
		Nil	73	98·6		Nil	192	78·7		Nil	9
		Total	74	100·0		Total	244	100·0		Total	9
1950	102	1	33	32·4	62	1	12	19·4	5	1	–
		2	8	7·8		2	3	4·8		2	1
		3	1	1·0		3	–	–		3	–
		4	–	–		4	1	1·6		4	–
		5	–	–		5	–	–		5	–
		Nil	60	58·8		Nil	46	74·2		Nil	4
		Total	102	100·0		Total	62	100·0		Total	5
1951	36	1	17	47·2	15	1	3	20·0	2	1	–
		2	5	13·9		2	–	–		2	–
		3	2	5·5		3	1	6·7		3	–
		4	–	–		4	–	–		4	–
		5	–	–		5	–	–		5	–

(Table continued on facing page)

Table 2.5 (continued)

Election date	Conservative				Labour				Other		
	Total MPs	Con-tests	No. MPs	%	Total MPs	Con-tests	No. MPs	%	Total MPs	Con-tests	No. MPs
1951		Nil	12	33·4		Nil	11	73·3		Nil	2
		Total	36	100·0		Total	15	100·0		Total	2
1955	78	1	19	24·4	26	1	7	26·9	2	1	–
		2	24	30·7		2	2	7·7		2	–
		3	6	7·7		3	2	7·7		3	–
		4	2	2·6		4	–	–		4	–
		5	–	–		5	–	–		5	–
		Nil	27	34·6		Nil	15	57·7		Nil	2
		Total	78	100·0		Total	26	100·0		Total	2
1959	104	1	34	32·7	42	1	5	11·9	1	1	1
		2	17	16·3		2	7	16·7		2	–
		3	3	2·9		3	2	4·8		3	–
		4	–	–		4	–	–		4	–
		5	–	–		5	–	–		5	–
		Nil	50	48·1		Nil	28	66·6		Nil	–
		Total	104	100·0		Total	42	100·0		Total	1
1964	64	1	20	31·2	106	1	31	29·2	6	1	–
		2	7	10·9		2	20	18·9		2	1
		3	1	1·5		3	5	4·7		3	1
		4	–	–		4	3	2·8		4	–
		5	–	–		5	1	0·9		5	–
		Nil	36	56·4		Nil	46	43·5		Nil	4
		Total	64	100·0		Total	106	100·0		Total	6
1966	13	1	3	23·1	72	1	29	40·3	5	1	4
		2	4	30·8		2	16	22·2		2	–
		3	–	–		3	5	6·9		3	–
		4	–	–		4	–	–		4	–
		5	–	–		5	–	–		5+	1
		Nil	6	46·1		Nil	22	30·6		Nil	–
		Total	13	100·0		Total	72	100·0		Total	5
1970	92	1	27	29·4	64	1	21	32·8	4	1	–
		2	22	23·9		2	8	12·5		2	–
		3	9	9·8		3	7	10·9		3	–
		4	–	–		4	1	1·6		4	–
		5	1	1·1		5	–	–		5	–
		Nil	33	35·8		Nil	27	42·2		Nil	4
		Total	92	100·0		Total	64	100·0		Total	4
Feb. 1974	62	1	27	43·6	46	1	16	35·8	21	1	6
		2	18	29·0		2	4	8·7		2	3
		3	–	–		3	1	2·2		3	–
		4	–	–		4	2	4·3		4	–
		5	–	–		5+	1	2·2		5	–
		Nil	17	27·4		Nil	22	47·8		Nil	12

(Table continued overleaf)

23

Table 2.5 (continued)

Election date	Conservative				Labour				Other		
	Total MPs	Con-tests	No. MPs	%	Total MPs	Con-tests	No. MPs	%	Total MPs	Con-tests	No. MPs
Feb. 1974		Total	62	100·0		Total	46	100·0		Total	21
Oct. 1974	8	1	3	37·5	22	1	11	50·0	7	1	4
		2	3	37·5		2	5	22·8		2	1
		3	–	–		3	3	13·6		3	–
		4	–	–		4	–	–		4	–
		5	–	–		5	–	–		5+	1
		Nil	2	25·0		Nil	3	13·6		Nil	1
		Total	8	100·0		Total	22	100·0		Total	7

finally succeeding declines rapidly. Only two Members were returned after being defeated on four previous occasions (both were elected in 1955, a year of Conservative victory), and just one Member found herself on the Conservative benches after suffering five earlier defeats at the polls (Table 2.4) [10]. Again this Member was returned in a year of Conservative victory.

Statistics about Labour Members in this period to a large extent suggest a similar story. Again the figures show that a greater proportion of Members of this party are suffering electoral defeat before their initial return to Parliament demonstrating it is a sustained trend. In 1945, 23 per cent of Labour MPs had contested seats before their first successful election and by October 1974, more than half of the Parliamentary Labour Party had needed more than one contest to secure their return to Westminster. At that election 52·9 per cent of Labour Members had been unsuccessful at their first election attempt. Although the magnitude of this trend is perhaps slightly less than in the Conservative Party, potential Labour parliamentarians are also apparently finding it that much more difficult to realise their political aspirations.

Similarly, the distribution of electoral experience in this party resembles that in the Conservative Party. The majority of those who were unsuccessful at their first attempt, did find success at their next contest: 21 per cent of Labour MPs succeeded at their second contest: 10·9 per cent were elected at their third attempt. The proportion who were elected after three or more defeats declined markedly. Only four MPs were returned after five or more earlier defeats – all on occasions when the Labour Party won the General Election. A mention must be made here of the current record-holder Neville Sandelson (Hillingdon, Hayes and Harlington) who was elected at the 1971 by-election on his ninth attempt. He had previously fought General Elections in 1950, 1951, 1955, 1959, 1966 and 1970, and by-elections in 1957 and 1967. His nearest rival is Gwynfer Evans, Plaid Cymru MP for Carmarthen. The president of his party since 1945, he fought six unsuccessful contests between 1945 and 1966, when he was finally returned to Parliament. Both men are evidence of the dictum that effort does eventually bring its just reward.

In looking at the electoral experiences of Members of Parliament since 1945, three clear features emerge. Firstly, there is a marked and sustained increase in the proportions of both major parties fighting unsuccessful contests prior to their initial return to Parliament. One survey which covered the period 1918—55 showed that 64·5 per cent of all Members in that period succeeded at their first contest [11]. The equivalent figure for the period 1945—74 is 59·5 per cent. In February 1974, for the first time, less than half of the House of Commons had succeeded at their first election contest. If nothing else, it suggests that there is healthy competition for winnable candidatures.

The second feature is the marked decline in the chances of eventual electoral success which comes with each subsequent defeat. One or two initial setbacks will not necessarily exclude all possibilities of a parliamentary career, but further defeats greatly reduce the chances of a long political life and, indeed, election to Parliament itself. There are willing contestants in all parties, but the men and women who may hope to make their mark in national politics are not generally those who needed a protracted struggle to enter the Commons.

The third feature, although less easily demonstrated in terms of aggregate data, is probably the most instructive. It is that although the general trend has clearly been towards more Members fighting unsuccessful contests before their final victory, this overall pattern does not apply equally to all candidates. This can be seen by concentrating on the successful newcomers at times of defeat for their party nationally. By definition new Members on these occasions will be contesting the better seats and it is notable that the incidence of previous defeats in both parties on these occasions is, generally, relatively lower. It must, of course, be stressed that this does not modify the major trend, but rather is a feature partially concealed within it. In simple terms it means that candidates fighting the safer seats often have less history of previous campaigns.

Experience of previous contests is not an important qualification for those who seek nominations in safe seats: indeed, it may even work against them. A selection committee may well prefer to choose their own, perhaps local, candidate, with whom they are able to establish closer identity than someone who is prepared to travel the country in search of a seat. Above all, in both parties the *right* kind of candidate is given priority. As Philip Buck has asserted, 'the easier and the younger a Member enters Parliament, the greater are his chances of a long career in Parliament and, with this, the reward of government office' [12]. If it is necessary to fight two or more elections before being returned, the likelihood of eventual government office declines greatly. The professional in politics, who becomes the parliamentary veteran, still finds relatively little difficulty in initially being elected to Parliament.

Notes

[1]   Ivor Crewe, Bo Sarlvik and James Alt, 'Partisan Dealignment in Britain 1964—

1974', *British Journal of Political Science*, Spring 1977. The authors comment on the brittle nature of electoral support for the Liberal Party.

[2]   Ibid. The demise of two party politics thesis receives as much attention in the serious press as it does in more academic publications.

[3]   See, for example, the establishment of a 'National Committee for Electoral Reform', and S.E. Finer (ed.), *Adversary Politics and Electoral Reform*, Anthony Wigram, London, 1975.

[4]   For discussion of the selection process see, A. Ranney, *Pathways to Parliament*, Macmillan, London, 1965, and M. Rush, *The Selection of Parliamentary Candidates*, Nelson, London, 1969. For a critical view, see P. Paterson, *The Selectorate*, MacGibbon and Kee, London, 1967.

[5]   The most common, and simplest, method is to average the percentage gain by one party and the percentage loss by the other major party.

[6]   A. Ranney, op. cit.

[7]   A.D.R. Dickinson, 'MPs' Readoption Conflicts', *Political Studies*, March 1975.

[8]   Harry Boardman, *Manchester Guardian*, 2 August 1945. Quoted in H.B. Berrington, *Backbench Opinion in the House of Commons 1945–55*, Pergamon, London, 1973.

[9]   'New' describes those Members winning their first general election. Where a Members enters Parliament by a by-election and then wins the subsequent general election, he is classified as 'new' at that general election.

[10] Mrs E. Kellett, returned in 1970.

[11] P.W. Buck, *Amateurs and Professionals in British Politics*, Chicago University Press, London, 1963.

[12] Ibid.

3 Age and generation

Introduction

It is not surprising to discover that Members of Parliament in this period are not representative of their electors in terms of their ages. Politics, like many other professions, is very much a middle-aged occupation. Indeed, many have argued that MPs are in general too old. The Labour Party, in particular, have traditionally operated a seniority principle, and often appeared to almost 'retire' loyal members of the movement to the House of Commons for the last decade or so of their active public life. Similarly, the Conservative Party apparently places considerable emphasis on business or professional success and this is taken into consideration in the selection of its parliamentary candidates. The result in both cases has generally been a neglect of youth and talent, at least to the extent that these two qualities are compatible, and a distinct preference for the senior and trusted. While this pattern has remained broadly true throughout these thirty years, there are a number of interesting nuances which combine to make the picture a little more complex.

Before looking at the predominant age patterns of MPs during these thirty years, it is appropriate to pause in order to consider the significance of studying age and generation. Electoral studies have stressed the importance of maturation in the acquisition, holding and later transmission of partisan allegiances amongst the electorate. These studies of political socialisation have especially concentrated upon the formative or adolescent years when political awareness first develops and the middle years when political interest increases and party attitudes strengthen [1]. It is, of course, during this latter period that the party allegiances of some of the more politically motivated will take on the positive form of seeking elected office.

In addition to firmer party commitment, election in early middle-age also allows the candidate to have experienced life outside Westminster. This appears important to both parties, but in different ways. The Conservatives still favour the 'balanced' parliamentarian — the Member who retains his outside interests and affairs and brings this knowledge and experience to bear upon parliamentary government. As Sir Winston Churchill observed thirty years ago:

> . . . Everybody here has private interests: some are directors of companies, some own property . . . Then there are those people who come to represent particular bodies, particular groups of a non-political character and there again we must recognise that as one of the conditions of our varied life. We are not supposed to be an assembly of gentlemen who have no interests of any kind and no association of any kind. That might happen in Heaven, but not, happily, here [2].

Retention of outside interests leads many Conservatives to resist the notion of the 'full-time' MP. On the Labour side, entry later in life facilitates a form of political apprenticeship. For many of the older Labour MPs election to Parliament was the reward for twenty or so years service to the Party because traditionally, in the Labour Party, theory has been no substitute for political experience and service.

By comparison, the younger a Member is elected, the more likely he is to be receptive to novel ideas and change. In his political stance he is more susceptible to liberal arguments, as studies of backbench opinion and attitudes to moral issues have indicated [3].

A further factor which should be considered here is the notion of political generation. Butler and Stokes have posited that generational influences contribute to the acquisition of partisan allegiances [4], and it seems not unreasonable to infer some effect on political activists. In the absence of any extensive research on this question, speculation can only be tentative but, given that there is generally a gap of two decades between the formation of political awareness and election to Parliament, it might be expected that a Member will display at that later time attitudes which developed in the earlier period. Thus, the new Labour recruits in 1945 had mostly been introduced to politics at a time of grave economic depression in the late 1920s and 1930s. It would have been very surprising if they had not reacted to such experiences in developing post-war welfare policies. Similarly, at the time that Labour next assumed power in 1964, there was an influx of MPs whose political awareness would have been forged against the backcloth of Attlee's Government and its welfare and nationalisation programmes. In addition, they would have been the recipients of the expanded educational opportunities afforded by the Butler Education Act. Both age and generation, then, have implications for the nature of parliamentary recruitment.

A middle-aged profession

In terms of recruitment, by far the largest proportion of Members are first elected to Parliament in their thirties and forties [5]. These two decades together account for just under 75 per cent of MPs at the time of their first election (Table 3.1). The difference between the parties is minimal and this obviously does reinforce the idea that, for most candidates parliamentary life is a second career. Given the precarious tenure involved in political life it is not surprising that most Members will desire to have established careers or made their mark elsewhere before they embark upon the process of getting elected to Parliament. From the viewpoint of those who select candidates, a prospective Conservative who has succeeded in the commercial world or a Labour man who has shown his political worth by an apprenticeship in trade union or municipal affairs might seem appropriate choices for their respective parties. In the absence of any formal training or qualifications available to prospective candidates, such experiences in the outside world might appear, as much as anything else, to be indicative of their suitability for party nomination.

Table 3.1
Age distribution of all Members, 1945–1974, on the
occasion of their first election

	Conservative		Labour		Other		Total	
	No.	%	No.	%	No.	%	No.	%
21–29	67	8·4	38	4·5	8	10·0	113	6·6
30–39	337	42·1	266	32·2	33	41·3	636	37·2
40–49	285	35·5	334	40·3	25	31·3	644	37·6
50–59	96	11·9	155	18·7	9	11·2	260	15·2
60–69	16	2·0	35	4·2	5	6·2	56	3·3
70+	1	0·1	1	0·1	–	–	2	0·1
Total	802	100.0	829	100·0	80	100·0	1711	100·0
INA	13		31		3		47	

Many fewer candidates, 18.6 per cent, are first elected after the age of fifty and even less after the age of sixty. Only two candidates since 1945 found themselves in the Commons for the first time after reaching seventy. In the older age group there is a distinction to be made between the Conservative and Labour parties. Nearly two-thirds of the Members first elected over the age of fifty were from the Labour Party. This does, of course, support the theory about parliamentary seats sometimes being employed as a form of reward to long-serving and devoted members of the Labour movement. At the other end of the scale, there are nearly twice as many Conservatives first elected in their twenties as there are in the Labour Party. The suggestion here seems to be that the Conservative Party is less reluctant to pick out prodigies at an early age. For a closer analysis it is appropriate to examine the patterns of change in the post-war period.

Patterns of change

In considering changes in the Conservative Party, it is helpful to separate the last two cohorts (February and October 1974) from the preceding eight. From 1945–70 there was some indication that the Conservative Party in Parliament was becoming older. Whilst changes in terms of age distribution were mainly limited to fluctuations in the 40–49 and 50–59 groups (which together form the bulk of the Party in any Parliament) up to 1970 there was a small but clear increase in the size of the latter group at the expense of the former (Table 3.2). That Conservative MPs were tending to be elected later in life is confirmed by the changing age distribution of new MPs up to and including the 1970 cohort (Table 3.3). However, this trend

Table 3.2
Age distribution of all Members

(a) Conservative

Age	1945 No. MPs	%	1950 No. MPs	%	1951 No. MPs	%	1955 No. MPs	%	1959 No. MPs	%
21−29	6	2·8	1	0·3	1	0·3	5	1·5	10	2·8
30−39	41	19·7	65	22·3	70	22·7	53	15·1	60	16·5
40−49	76	36·6	118	40·3	115	36·6	119	35·1	137	37·7
50−59	46	22·1	71	24·3	93	29·6	119	35·1	120	33·1
60−69	31	14·9	28	9·4	26	8·3	37	10·9	32	8·8
70+	8	3·9	10	3·4	8	2·5	6	1·8	4	1·1
Total	208	100·0	293	100·0	313	100·0	339	100·0	363	100·0
INA	5		4		7		4		2	

Age	1964 No. MPs	%	1966 No. MPs	%	1970 No. MPs	%	Feb. 1974 No. MPs	%	Oct. 1974 No. MPs	%
21−29	3	1·0	1	0·4	2	0·6	2	0·7	3	1·1
30−39	52	17·3	38	15·1	49	15·0	47	16·0	48	17·5
40−49	90	30·0	84	33·3	126	38·6	113	38·4	111	40·3
50−59	104	34·7	90	35·7	110	33·9	91	31·0	80	29·1
60−69	48	16·0	38	15·1	37	11·3	38	12·9	32	11·6
70+	3	1·0	1	0·4	2	0·6	3	1·0	1	0·4
Total	300	100·0	252	100·0	326	100·0	294	100·0	275	100·0
INA	1		1		4		3		2	

(b) Labour

Age	1945 No. MPs	%	1950 No. MPs	%	1951 No. MPs	%	1955 No. MPs	%	1959 No. MPs	%
21−29	7	1·9	–	–	2	0·7	–	–	1	0·4
30−39	70	18·8	38	12·2	31	10·6	22	7·7	17	6·6
40−49	110	29·6	94	30·2	92	31·6	69	25·4	59	22·9
50−59	103	27·7	93	29·9	84	28·7	104	38·3	102	39·8
60−69	67	18·0	76	24·5	75	25·7	60	22·0	59	22·9
70+	15	4·0	10	3·2	8	2·7	18	6·6	19	7·4
Total	372	100·0	311	100·0	292	100·0	273	100·0	257	100·0
INA	28		4		3		4		1	

Age	1964 No. MPs	%	1966 No. MPs	%	1970 No. MPs	%	Feb. 1974 No. MPs	%	Oct. 1974 No. MPs	%
21−29	1	0·3	6	1·7	5	1·7	2	0·7	4	1·3
30−39	43	13·6	67	18·5	45	15·8	39	13·0	50	15·8
40−49	78	24·8	98	27·0	88	30·5	96	32·2	104	32·7
50−59	105	33·4	102	28·2	80	27·8	93	31·1	94	29·7
60−69	71	22·5	72	19·9	63	21·8	62	20·7	58	18·3
70+	17	5·4	17	4·7	7	2·4	7	2·3	7	2·2

(Table continued on facing page)

Table 3.2 (continued)

Age	1964 No. MPs	%	1966 No. MPs	%	1970 No. MPs	%	Feb. 1974 No. MPs	%	Oct. 1974 No. MPs	%
Total	315	100·0	362	100·0	288	100·0	299	100·0	317	100·0
INA	5		3		2		2		2	

(c) Others

Age	1945	1950	1951	1955	1959	1964	1966	1970	Feb. 1974	Oct. 1974
21–29	–	–	–	2	–	–	1	1	1	2
30–39	4	4	4	–	1	4	6	4	12	13
40–49	7	4	3	5	4	2	3	3	14	15
50–59	5	1	–	1	1	2	1	2	9	7
60–69	7	3	2	1	–	1	1	–	1	2
70+	1	1	1	1	1	–	–	–	–	–
Total	24	13	10	10	7	9	12	10	37	39
INA	3	0	0	0	0	0	0	0	0	0

Table 3.3
Age distribution of new Members

(a) Conservative

Age	Pre-1945 No. MPs	%	1945 No. MPs	%	1950 No. MPs	%	1951 No. MPs	%	1955 No. MPs	%	1959 No. MPs	%
21–29	35	19·9	6	8·3	1	1·0	1	2·8	5	6·5	10	9·6
30–39	76	43·2	28	38·9	44	43·2	15	44·2	27	35·1	39	37·5
40–49	40	22·7	25	34·8	41	40·2	11	32·4	29	37·7	43	41·3
50–59	17	9·7	8	11·1	16	15·6	5	14·7	15	19·4	11	10·6
60–69	7	4·0	5	6·9	–	–	2	5·9	1	1·3	1	1·0
70+	1	0·5	–	–	–	–	–	–	–	–	–	–
Total	176	100·0	72	100·0	102	100·0	34	100·0	77	100·0	104	100·0
INA	6		2		0		2		1		0	

Age	1964 No. MPs	%	1966 No. MPs	%	1970 No. MPs	%	Feb.1974 No. MPs	%	Oct.1974 No. MPs	%
21–29	3	4·7	–	–	2	2·2	2	3·2	2	25·0
30–39	32	50·0	5	38·5	37	41·2	32	51·7	2	25·0
40–49	20	31·2	6	46·1	40	44·4	26	41·9	4	50·0
50–59	9	14·1	2	15·4	11	12·2	2	3·2	–	–
60–69	–	–	–	–	–	–	–	–	–	–

(Table continued overleaf)

Table 3.3 (continued)

Age	1964 No. MPs	%	1966 No. MPs	%	1970 No. MPs	%	Feb. 1974 No. MPs	%	Oct. 1974 No. MPs	%
70+	–	–	–	–	–	–	–	–	–	–
Total	64	100·0	13	100·0	90	100·0	62	100·0	8	100·0
INA	0		0		2		0		0	

(b) Labour

Age	Pre-1945 No. MPs	%	1945 No. MPs	%	1950 No. MPs	%	1951 No. MPs	%	1955 No. MPs	%	1959 No. MPs	%
21–29	10	6·7	7	3·1	1	1·6	2	13·3	1	4·2	1	2·4
30–39	37	24·7	66	29·1	18	29·0	3	20·0	6	25·0	9	21·4
40–49	70	46·7	88	38·7	23	37·2	8	53·4	10	41·7	18	42·8
50–59	29	19·2	44	19·4	17	27·4	2	13·3	7	29·1	13	31·0
60–69	4	2·7	21	9·3	3	4·8	–	–	–	–	1	2·4
70+	–	–	1	0·4	–	–	–	–	–	–	–	–
Total	150	100·0	227	100·0	62	100·0	15	100·0	24	100·0	42	100·0
INA	11		17		0		0		2		0	

Age	1964 No. MPs	%	1966 No. MPs	%	1970 No. MPs	%	Feb. 1974 No. MPs	%	Oct. 1974 No. MPs	%
21–29	1	0·9	7	9.7	5	7·8	1	2·2	2	9·0
30–39	36	34·3	34	47·2	28	43·7	19	41·3	10	45·5
40–49	48	45·7	23	32·0	23	36·0	15	32·6	8	36·5
50–59	19	18·2	5	6·9	8	12·5	9	19·6	2	9·0
60–69	1	0·9	3	4·2	–	–	2	4·3	–	–
70+	–	–	–	–	–	–	–	–	–	–
Total	105	100·0	72	100·0	64	100·0	46	100·0	22	100·0
INA	1		0		0		0		0	

(c) Others

Age	Pre-1945	1945	1950	1951	1955	1959	1964	1966	1970	Feb. 1974	Oct. 1974
21–29	2	–	–	–	2	–	–	1	1	1	1
30–39	6	4	2	1	–	1	3	2	1	10	3
40–49	7	2	2	1	–	–	2	2	1	6	2
50–59	3	–	–	–	–	–	–	–	1	4	1
60–69	1	2	1	–	–	–	1	–	–	–	–
70+	–	–	–	–	–	–	–	–	–	–	–
Total	19	8	5	2	2	1	6	5	4	21	7
INA	2	1	0	0	0	0	0	0	0	0	0

reverses with the last two cohorts. The Conservative MPs elected in October 1974 includes the smallest proportion of Members in their fifties and the largest proportion in their forties since the General Election of 1950. The group of new Members in this party who were returned in the February election includes the largest proportion of those in their thirties at any election in this thirty year period. Any trend towards a slightly more elderly Conservative Member was firmly halted in 1974 when there was a fresh intake of more youthful colleagues.

In comparison with the Conservative Party the Labour Party has consistently returned a more elderly group to Westminster. Once again the majority of Members have been aged between 40 and 59 years, but it is significant that in this party the dominance of these two decades is relatively closely matched by the 60—69 age group. At all but three elections the proportion of Labour Members aged between 60 and 69 has been something in excess of 20 per cent, whilst the equivalent proportion on the Conservative side of the House has been nearer 12 per cent. Even the proportion of Labour Members aged 70 years and over, whilst relatively small and declining from its peak in 1959, has been significantly larger than the proportion of Conservatives in this age range. As would be expected the size of the 21—29 age group has been consistently small and has never risen above its 1945 figure of seven Members, 1·9 per cent of the PLP at that time.

Amongst new Labour MPs, the age range 40—49 dominated until the 1966 General Election. From that election, the intake of new Labour Members has contained a greater proportion of its number who were in their thirties than those who were in their forties. In comparison, the proportion of new Labour recruits under 30 years of age has remained small throughout, and the figures suggest that usually the youngest candidates are not chosen for the safest seats. There is a tendency for the proportion of new recruits in their twenties to decline when their party loses a general election. In contrast to this, the age range 50—59 seems to benefit in times of national defeat. The implication here is that potential candidates in their fifties are looked upon with some favour by selection committees in the safe constituencies. It is apparent that this group consists largely of those members of the party who have worked their way through the movement, have completed their political apprenticeship and are now rewarded with a safe parliamentary seat for the remaining ten years or so of their political career.

The peculiar position of the minor party representatives is reflected in their ages and of the parliamentary groupings they have the youngest profile. Because of their number, it would be inappropriate to refer to percentages, but it is clear that these Members do generally find themselves at Westminster somewhat earlier in life than their Conservative or Labour counterparts. This is especially true following the Nationalist victories at the last two general elections. In addition, they may also assume positions of leadership in their party at relatively tender ages. But their position is not without its disadvantages: in comparison with their colleagues in the major parties, they tend to retire from parliamentary life much younger, and not usually voluntarily [6].

The overall result of these trends, although slight, may also be viewed in terms of average ages which, in effect, present a simplified version of the changes which have occurred in the patterns of age distribution. Over these thirty years, the average age of all the 1,758 MPs at the time of first entry to the Commons was 41·7 years. Throughout, this figure has been lower in the Conservative Party than it has in the Labour Party. Taking the period as a whole, average age at initial election was 40·9 years for Conservatives and 42·5 years for Labour. Amongst Conservatives, the equivalent figure for the complete parliamentary party following any election varies between 47·8 and 49·5 years. On the Labour side, the range is 49·5 to 54·9 years (Table 3.4).

Table 3.4

Average ages of MPs 1945–1974, by type and cohort

(a) Conservative

Type of Member	Pre-1945	1945	1950	1951	1955	1959	1964	1966	1970	Feb. 1974	Oct. 1974
All	–	48·4	47·8	47·8	48·9	47·8	49·4	49·4	49·5	48·8	47·8
New	38·2	41·6	42·7	42·0	41·7	39·9	40·1	41·5	41·2	39·1	36·6
Departing	–	57·3	53·2	54·5	54·8	51·8	57·5	61·5	57·1	52·9	–

(b) Labour

Type of Member	Pre-1945	1945	1950	1951	1955	1959	1964	1966	1970	Feb. 1974	Oct. 1974
All	–	49·5	51·9	52·3	54·9	54·7	52·3	51·2	51·2	51·0	49·9
New	43·4	46·0	45·1	41·9	44·0	45·4	43·5	39·9	39·6	42·3	38·5
Departing	–	55·1	54·8	59·2	60·4	62·7	63·5	54·2	61·0	56·4	–

(c) Others

Type of Member	Pre-1945	1945	1950	1951	1955	1959	1964	1966	1970	Feb. 1974	Oct. 1974
All	–	50·8	49·7	48·4	44·7	49·0	43·7	41·3	40·0	44·3	43·0
New	42·4	42·6	46·0	39·0	23·0	30·0	42·0	39·0	39·3	41·0	38·1
Departing	–	53·5	50·0	57·5	39·5	55·5	48·0	45·2	28·5	50·2	–

Between 1955 and 1974, the average ages of Conservative groups tended to increase, but at the two elections of that year, there was a distinct fall. The average age of the October 1974 group equalled the lowest in this period. This reversal is shown even more clearly in the ages of new recruits at the 1974 General Elections, when the average on both occasions fell below 40 years. (The October figure should perhaps be treated with a little caution since it represents only 8 Conservatives.)

The Labour figures provide evidence to suggest two themes. Firstly, the average age tends to be higher when the party is in Opposition: the two highest averages were in 1955 and 1959. Secondly, the average age of Labour Members, which reached its peak in 1955, is falling. By October 1974 this average had dropped to 49·9 years, only just higher than it had been after the Labour landslide of 1945. The average age of new Labour MPs on this occasion is even more notable: at 38·5 years, it is comfortably the lowest in this period. Taken together with the intakes of 1966 and 1970 (especially significant since Labour lost this election), they clearly suggest not only a younger parliamentary party but also changes in the types of candidates chosen. Indeed, the 1966 and 1970 new intakes were actually younger than their Conservative counterparts.

Conclusion

Writing shortly after the 1955 election, J.F.S. Ross noted that 'We can safely say that the gap between the average ages of the two dominant parliamentary parties shows no sign of disappearing' [7]. From the information then available, Ross was no doubt justified in this observation but it is no longer appropriate to draw the same conclusion. The gap in average ages in 1955 was exactly six years and it is now just over two years. Of course, neither party is particularly youthful but, over the last five elections in particular, there has been an unmistakable drift towards younger Labour Members. It is important to understand both the cause and effect of this process.

At the outset, it must be repeated that despite these changes, Parliament continues to be dominated by men and women in their middle-ages. It is natural that this should be so. Parties will require some indication of the worth of candidates before they select them and individuals will generally desire to have established themselves in their career before they seek nomination. There is a further possible explanation which is that greater partisanship or political commitment usually comes with later life. This is not to say that age itself leads to stronger political attachments, but that age allows for a longer association with one party which does bring more pronounced durability of political views [8]. On the candidate's part, therefore, middle-age produces more career opportunity and engenders greater political commitment.

In terms of age, the Conservative profile has changed little during these years. It is usual for political recruitment in predominantly middle class parties to take place earlier than in other parties and this practice has obtained in the context of advancement to the House of Commons. Indeed, for some Conservatives the pathway to the House has been especially short. In his work on the social structure of eighteenth century British politics, Sir Lewis Namier described the importance of family political traditions.

> For several centuries the dream of English youth and manhood of the nation forming class has remained unchanged; it has been fixed and focused on the House of Commons, a modified, socialised arena for battles, drive and dominion [9].

He quotes a passage from a letter written by Lord Chesterfield to his son in 1749:

> You will be of the House of Commons as soon as you are of age, and you must first make a figure there if you would make a figure in your country.

Whilst the inevitable parliament men and great political dynasties are less evident now than they were then, or even just fifty years ago, breeding and family political traditions continue to facilitate the political advancement of aspiring Conservative parliamentarians. Especially for those with the conventional public school/Oxbridge background, party nomination may still be found rather early in life.

As the figures suggest, the Labour Party has generally proven disposed to adopt older candidates in its better constituencies. Usually, these candidates are drawn from the working class, and they, more than people from higher social strata, have needed the extra time prior to nomination in order to establish their prominence and influence in the local party. In working class groups, age or seniority is a frequenty source of rank. Such candidates are less likely to travel in search of nomination and tend to be more locally orientated — both in terms of seeking a parliamentary vacancy and, if elected, in concentrating upon their constituency duties as a Member of Parliament. This emphasis on being *local* MPs is facilitated by the fact that, since they are elected in later life, they stand less chance of achieving government office during their stay at Westminster and the representation of a locality, or particular interests in the case of trade union seats, might prove appealing to selection committees. Nomination at a later age also carries the advantage of being able to rotate the candidature through a larger number of MPs [10]. The fact, therefore, that the Labour Party is recruiting younger MPs portends less opportunities for working class candidates. Younger Labour recruits imply new sources and types of Labour MPs.

Notes

[1]   D. Butler and D. Stokes, *Political Change in Britain*, 1st ed., Penguin, London, 1971, Ch. 3.

[2]   Committee of Privileges, 1947.

[3]   S.E. Finer, H.B. Berrington, D.J. Bartholomew, *Backbench Opinion in the House of Commons 1955–59*, Pergamon, London, 1961, p. 117, and P.G. Richards, *Parliament and Conscience*, Allen & Unwin, London, 1970, Ch. 9.

[4]   Butler and Stokes, op. cit., pp. 86–9.

[5]   Throughout this Chapter, 'thirties' refers to those Members aged 30 years to 39 years 11 months, and 'forties' to those aged 40 years to 49 years 11 months etc.

[6]   There are, of course, exceptions. For example, J. Grimond (1950–   ); J. Thorpe (1959–   ); R. Bowen (1945–66).

[7]   J.F.S. Ross, *Elections and Electors*, Eyre and Spottiswoode, London, 1955, p. 399.

[8]   See D. Butler and D. Stokes, op. cit., pp. 78–86.
[9]   L.B. Namier, *The Structure of Politics at the Accession of George III*, London, 1929, p. 2.
[10] R.W. Johnson, 'The British Political Elite, 1955–1972', *European Journal of Sociology*, 1973, p. 62.

4 The educational background of MPs

Introduction

Whilst no direct attempt has been made in this study to identify the actual social class origins of MPs [1], the education which they receive prior to election, more than any other feature, indicates the background from which Members come. Education provides, besides the more obvious training in academic skills, the no less important social values and attitudes which adolescents adopt and generally retain through their adult life. Social status and contacts are added to this in the case of those schoolchildren who are fortunate enough to receive their education outside the state system. Public school education is a reasonable guide to class origins, if only because 'the cost of it makes it a clear prerogative of the well-to-do' [2]. The abundance of public school men in the House of Commons must, therefore, be taken to mean that these people are from upper middle class backgrounds. Education is also perhaps the most significant single criterion for examining the difference between the two parties. Although the process of embourgeoisement in the Labour Party is unmistakable, the new middle class Labour recruits do not follow identical educational routes to their middle class Conservative colleagues. Indeed, a common vindication of the middle classes replacing the working classes in the PLP is expressed in terms of an ascending Labour meritocracy who rise through effort and ability rather than breeding [3].

Before looking at the educational profiles of the parliamentary parties during these thirty years it is appropriate to say something about the classifications which are used here. The system employed is an augmented version of the one which appears in the Nuffield series. The two most important additions to that system are the inclusion of slightly more detailed categories, notably *private* and *service college*, and an entirely new category *professional* [4]. Private schools are those fee-paying independent schools which are not ranked as public schools and a service college is one of the officer training colleges attached to one of the three defence services. The Nuffield series uses 'elementary plus' or 'secondary plus' categories to classify all those Members who, after leaving school, subsequently received some technical or adult training. The present study has retained these categories to classify those Members, almost all of whom were Labour, who received non-vocational adult training, but included professional to describe those who received such as legal or non-university teacher training after leaving school which ultimately led to an occupation which would normally be classified as a profession.

Recruitment studies inevitably emphasise the importance of public schools, and to most foreigners it always appears ironical that the British describe those schools which are least accessible to the general public as public schools. It might be worthwhile, therefore, at this stage to define the use of the term 'public school' in this particular study. It is taken to mean those schools which are members of the Headmasters' Conference, the Governing Bodies Association or the equivalent for girls' schools, the Governing Bodies of the Girls' Schools Association. In the main these are independent boarding schools receiving no grants from public funds, but they do include a few other schools, mainly direct grant grammar schools, which are not independent of the state school system. Rather than differentiate between these two types, they are all described as public schools. Conversely, fee-paying independent schools which are not represented on these bodies are simply described as private schools.

MPs are, like most of us, complicated characters and it is not easy to simplify all the possible permutations of educational training which are available to schoolchildren and students. It is therefore obviously necessary to settle for some acceptable compromise between vagueness and complexity.

Conservatives: the patrician tradition

In choosing their parliamentary candidates, the Conservative Party consistently concern themselves more with rank and achievement than party political experience. Breeding and educational attainment are customarily seen as the two most important qualifications in this party for recruitment to the political élite [5]. The former is normally demonstrated by a public school background and the latter by graduation from one of the two ancient universities of Oxford or Cambridge. And whilst there have been some minor adjustments to this traditional picture of an exclusive patrician class, especially in view of the backgrounds of the last two Conservative leaders, it is a description which has remained largely true through these thirty years. In common with all predominantly middle class parties, Conservatives select as their candidates the younger and more educationally qualified. This applies equally to legislative recruitment and later advancement to ministerial positions.

Most MPs during this period attended one of three types of school — elementary, secondary or public. Elementary schools were board or council schools of a nonselective type which existed before the 1944 Education Act. Not surprisingly, the education of only eight Conservatives was limited to this minimum of schooling (Table 4.1). Even amongst the secondary school element, there are relatively few Conservatives to be found. Since 1945, only 17·1 per cent of all Conservative MPs have been educated in secondary or grammar schools and of these most followed their secondary school education by a place at university, most frequently Oxford or Cambridge. Thus if such candidates were unable to meet the public school qualification which selection committees prefer, they were able to 'normalise' their educational background by their term at one of the older universities. There is some suggestion that the incidence of secondary school/university Conservative

MPs has tended to increase (Tables 4.2 and 4.3). But this trend is slight, and there is evidence that when the electoral pendulum swings against the Conservative Party, the proportion of these types remaining at Westminster decreases.

Table 4.1
Education of all MPs, 1945–1974

	Con	Lab	Other	Total	per cent
Elementary only	6	173	2	181	(16·2)
Elementary +	2	94	1	97	
Secondary only	43	87	10	140	
Secondary +	–	33	1	34	
Secondary/professional	19	68	7	94	
Secondary/university	73	231	24	328	(19·1)
Secondary/service college	–	–	1	1	
Secondary/service/university	1	–	–	1	
Private only	10	2	1	13	
Private/service college	13	1	–	14	
Private/university	5	–	–	5	
Private/service/university	3	–	1	4	
Private/professional	1	1	–	2	
Public only	111	19	6	136	
Public/professional	39	7	2	48	
Public/service college	48	2	–	50	
Public/'Oxbridge'	372	87	15	474	(27·6)
Public/other university	49	39	7	95	
Foreign/UK university	–	2	–	2	
Abroad	1	–	–	1	
INA	19	14	5	38	
Total	815	860	83	1758	
All public schools	619	154	30	803	(46·7)
Eton	165	8	2	175	(10·2)
Oxford	225	90	11	326	
Cambridge	180	47	8	235	(32·7)
London	24	75	1	100	
Wales	5	25	7	37	
Scotland	19	43	14	76	
Ireland	11	3	2	16	
Foreign	9	7	–	16	
Other universities	30	69	4	103	
All universities	503	359	47	909	(52·8)

It is rather symbolic that the contest for the leadership of the Conservative Party following Harold Macmillan's retirement in 1963 was fought between two traditional Conservative patricians, Lord Home and Lord Hailsham: both had the classic Eton and Christ Church, Oxford, background. Just over a decade later the leadership contest was fought between two rather different breeds of Conservatives, Edward Heath and Margaret Thatcher: both are from middle class business families and are grammar school products [6].

Table 4.2
Education of all MPs, by election

	1945 Con	1945 Lab	1945 Oth	1950 Con	1950 Lab	1950 Oth	1951 Con	1951 Lab	1951 Oth
Elementary only	1	117	1	3	81	–	3	69	–
Elementary +	–	49	1	–	47	–	–	46	–
Secondary only	7	40	2	13	27	1	16	31	2
Secondary +	–	4	–	–	6	–	–	7	–
Secondary/professional	4	26	3	4	21	1	5	14	–
Secondary/university	15	72	9	18	58	5	22	55	4
Secondary/service college	–	–	–	–	–	1	–	–	–
Secondary/service/univ.	–	–	–	–	–	–	–	–	–
Private only	3	1	–	5	1	–	5	1	–
Private/service college	2	1	–	3	1	–	5	1	–
Private/university	1	–	–	1	–	–	1	–	–
Private/service/university	–	–	–	–	–	–	–	–	–
Private/professional	1	1	–	1	–	–	–	–	–
Public only	24	10	3	33	9	1	36	10	1
Public/professional	3	3	1	7	1	–	9	–	–
Public/service college	27	2	–	32	–	–	29	–	–
Public/'Oxbridge'	102	41	7	150	39	2	157	40	2
Public/other university	13	19	–	18	20	–	19	18	1
Foreign/UK university	–	–	–	–	–	–	–	–	–
Abroad	–	–	–	1	–	–	1	–	–
INA	10	14	–	8	4	2	12	3	–
Total	213	400	27	297	315	13	320	295	10
All public schools	169	75	11	240	69	2	216	68	4
Eton	55	6	–	77	4	1	75	4	1
Oxford	62	36	6	94	33	1	99	34	1
Cambridge	46	20	3	62	15	2	68	15	2
London	3	25	1	8	17	–	8	14	–
Wales	1	8	3	–	9	4	1	8	3
Scotland	10	16	2	7	16	–	7	16	–
Ireland	3	3	–	3	3	–	2	2	–
Foreign	3	4	–	3	4	–	4	3	–
Other universities	3	20	1	10	20	–	10	21	1
All universities	131	132	16	187	117	7	199	113	7

	1955 Con	1955 Lab	1955 Oth	1959 Con	1959 Lab	1959 Oth	1964 Con	1964 Lab	1964 Oth
Elementary only	3	62	1	3	51	–	2	56	–
Elementary +	2	42	–	2	41	–	1	38	–
Secondary only	20	32	–	24	30	–	16	33	1
Secondary +	–	6	–	–	4	–	–	9	–
Secondary/professional	7	16	–	11	13	–	8	25	–
Secondary/university	23	51	4	30	52	2	24	78	3
Secondary/service college	–	–	–	–	–	–	–	–	–
Secondary/service/univ.	1	–	–	1	–	–	–	–	–

(Table continued overleaf)

Table 4.2 (continued)

	1955			1959			1964		
	Con	Lab	Oth	Con	Lab	Oth	Con	Lab	Oth
Private only	6	1	–	3	1	–	3	1	1
Private/service college	6	1	–	9	1	–	6	1	–
Private/university	–	–	–	2	–	–	3	–	–
Private/service/university	1	–	–	1	–	–	2	–	–
Private/professional	–	–	–	–	–	–	–	–	–
Public only	37	8	1	49	11	1	40	11	–
Public/professional	9	2	–	19	3	–	16	4	–
Public/service college	26	–	–	21	–	–	15	–	–
Public/'Oxbridge'	171	36	2	168	33	3	147	41	3
Public/other university	21	18	1	17	16	1	14	20	1
Foreign/UK university	–	–	–	–	–	–	–	–	–
Abroad	1	–	–	1	–	–	1	–	–
INA	9	2	1	4	2	–	3	3	–
Total	343	277	10	365	258	7	301	320	9
All public schools	264	64	4	274	63	5	232	76	4
Eton	75	3	1	70	2	2	66	2	2
Oxford	106	30	1	104	32	2	88	36	4
Cambridge	74	15	2	79	12	2	74	20	–
London	9	20	–	8	21	–	4	29	–
Wales	1	6	3	2	4	1	2	7	2
Scotland	8	12	–	6	13	–	4	15	1
Ireland	4	1	–	5	1	–	4	1	–
Foreign	5	1	–	5	1	–	1	2	–
Other universities	10	20	1	10	17	1	13	29	–
All universities	217	105	7	219	101	6	190	139	7

	1966			1970			Feb. 1974		
	Con	Lab	Oth	Con	Lab	Oth	Con	Lab	Oth
Elementary only	3	54	–	4	33	–	3	32	–
Elementary +	–	39	–	–	31	–	–	24	–
Secondary only	10	36	1	21	25	1	20	24	5
Secondary +	–	13	–	–	13	–	–	21	1
Secondary/professional	6	28	–	11	31	2	7	34	3
Secondary/university	23	108	1	33	99	2	34	117	9
Secondary/service college	–	–	–	–	–	–	–	–	–
Secondary/service/univ.	–	–	–	–	–	–	–	–	–
Private only	2	1	1	3	–	–	2	–	–
Private/service college	2	1	–	3	–	–	3	–	–
Private/university	2	–	–	4	–	–	2	–	–
Private/service/university	2	–	1	3	–	–	3	–	–
Private/professional	–	–	–	–	–	–	–	–	–
Public only	38	11	–	51	5	–	43	3	4
Public/professional	15	4	–	17	3	–	18	3	–
Public/service college	7	–	–	8	–	–	2	–	–
Public/'Oxbridge'	130	46	5	147	37	3	143	29	7
Public/other university	12	22	3	21	11	2	16	12	6

(Table continued on facing page)

Table 4.2. (continued)

	1966			1970			Feb. 1974		
	Con	Lab	Oth	Con	Lab	Oth	Con	Lab	Oth
Foreign/UK university	–	–	–	–	1	–	–	1	–
Abroad	–	–	–	1	–	–	–	–	–
INA	1	2	–	3	1	–	1	1	2
Total	253	365	12	330	290	10	297	301	37
All public schools	199	83	8	243	56	5	222	47	17
Eton	56	3	2	62	2	2	54	1	2
Oxford	80	43	3	93	38	2	89	38	5
Cambridge	64	27	3	75	21	1	76	20	2
London	4	36	–	12	30	–	10	34	–
Wales	2	9	1	3	11	1	4	13	2
Scotland	3	20	2	2	17	2	4	17	8
Ireland	3	1	–	4	–	1	1	–	2
Foreign	1	3	–	2	1	–	3	1	–
Other universities	12	37	1	17	30	–	11	36	3
All universities	169	176	10	208	148	7	198	159	22

	Oct. 1974		
	Con	Lab	Oth
Elementary only	3	30	–
Elementary +	–	21	–
Secondary only	17	27	6
Secondary +	–	22	1
Secondary/professional	7	36	3
Secondary/university	33	128	13
Secondary/service college	–	–	–
Secondary/service/univ.	–	–	–
Private only	2	–	–
Private/service college	3	–	–
Private/university	2	–	–
Private/service/university	3	–	–
Private/professional	–	–	–
Public only	39	2	2
Public/professional	17	3	1
Public/service college	2	–	–
Public/'Oxbridge'	131	33	6
Public/other university	17	14	5
Foreign/UK university	–	2	–
Abroad	–	–	–
INA	1	1	2
Total	277	319	39
All public schools	206	52	14
Eton	47	1	–
Oxford	76	42	4
Cambridge	76	24	3
London	11	35	–

(Table continued overleaf)

Table 4.2 (continued)

| | Oct. 1974 | | |
	Con	Lab	Oth
Wales	4	11	3
Scotland	5	19	11
Ireland	–	–	2
Foreign	3	2	–
Other universities	11	44	1
All universities	186	177	24

Table 4.3
Education of new MPs, by election

| | Pre-1945 | | | 1945 | | | 1950 | | |
	Con	Lab	Oth	Con	Lab	Oth	Con	Lab	Oth
Elementary only	–	57	1	1	60	–	2	12	–
Elementary +	–	19	–	–	30	1	–	9	–
Secondary only	3	12	3	4	28	–	8	3	–
Secondary +	–	2	–	–	2	–	–	4	–
Secondary/professional	2	8	2	2	18	1	1	5	–
Secondary/university	16	27	5	2	46	4	9	12	1
Secondary/service college	–	–	–	–	–	–	–	–	1
Secondary/service/univ.	–	–	–	–	–	–	–	–	–
Private only	4	1	–	–	–	–	1	–	–
Private/service college	–	–	–	3	1	–	1	–	–
Private/university	1	–	–	–	–	–	–	–	–
Private/service/university	–	–	–	–	–	–	–	–	–
Private/professional	–	–	–	1	1	–	–	–	–
Public only	15	7	2	13	4	1	12	2	–
Public/professional	4	–	1	–	3	–	5	–	–
Public/service college	19	1	–	10	1	–	7	–	–
Public/'Oxbridge'	101	15	4	30	29	2	44	10	2
Public/other university	11	5	1	3	14	–	7	5	–
Foreign/UK university	–	–	–	–	–	–	–	–	–
Abroad	–	–	–	–	–	–	1	–	–
INA	6	7	2	5	7	–	4	–	1
Total	182	161	21	74	244	9	102	62	5
All public schools	150	28	8	56	49	3	75	17	2
Eton	49	4	–	18	2	–	21	–	1
Oxford	64	10	5	18	30	1	25	10	1
Cambridge	44	8	2	11	12	1	21	2	1
London	4	8	–	–	17	1	4	4	–
Wales	–	4	1	1	4	2	–	3	1
Scotland	10	9	1	1	7	1	1	4	–
Ireland	3	–	–	–	3	–	2	–	–
Foreign	1	1	–	2	3	–	1	–	–
Other universities	3	7	1	2	13	–	6	4	–
All universities	129	47	10	35	89	6	60	27	3

Table 4.3 (continued)

	1951			1955			1959		
	Con	Lab	Oth	Con	Lab	Oth	Con	Lab	Oth
Elementary only	–	3	–	1	2	1	–	8	–
Elementary +	–	–	–	2	5	–	–	11	–
Secondary only	4	4	1	5	5	–	6	6	–
Secondary +	–	1	–	–	1	–	–	–	–
Secondary/professional	1	1	–	3	2	–	5	1	–
Secondary/university	4	4	–	6	7	–	10	11	–
Secondary/service college	–	–	–	–	–	–	–	–	–
Secondary/service/univ.	–	–	–	1	–	–	–	–	–
Private only	–	–	–	3	–	–	2	–	–
Private/service college	2	–	–	1	–	–	3	–	–
Private/university	–	–	–	–	–	–	2	–	–
Private/service/university	–	–	–	1	–	–	–	–	–
Private/professional	–	–	–	–	–	–	–	–	–
Public only	4	–	–	10	–	–	20	3	–
Public/professional	2	–	–	1	2	–	11	–	–
Public/service college	2	–	–	3	–	–	1	–	–
Public/'Oxbridge'	14	1	–	35	2	–	41	1	1
Public/other university	–	1	1	6	–	–	3	1	–
Foreign/UK university	–	–	–	–	–	–	–	–	–
Abroad	–	–	–	–	–	–	–	–	–
INA	3	–	–	–	–	1	–	–	–
Total	36	15	2	78	26	2	104	42	1
All public schools	22	2	1	55	4	–	76	5	1
Eton	8	–	–	16	–	–	17	–	1
Oxford	11	1	–	20	2	–	30	1	1
Cambridge	6	1	–	17	–	–	17	1	–
London	–	–	–	3	5	–	–	7	–
Wales	1	1	–	–	–	–	1	–	–
Scotland	–	1	–	1	–	–	2	3	–
Ireland	–	–	–	2	–	–	2	–	–
Foreign	–	–	–	3	–	–	1	–	–
Other universities	–	2	1	3	2	–	3	1	–
All universities	18	6	1	49	9	0	56	13	1

	1964			1966			1970		
	Con	Lab	Oth	Con	Lab	Oth	Con	Lab	Oth
Elementary only	1	18	–	–	5	–	1	4	–
Elementary +	–	9	–	–	5	–	–	4	–
Secondary only	1	7	1	1	6	–	9	7	1
Secondary +	–	6	–	–	5	–	–	3	–
Secondary/professional	1	13	–	–	5	–	3	9	2
Secondary/university	6	31	2	1	35	–	12	28	1
Secondary/service college	–	–	–	–	–	–	–	–	–
Secondary/service/univ.	–	–	–	–	–	–	–	–	–
Private only	–	1	1	–	–	–	–	–	–

(Table continued overleaf)

45

Table 4.3 (continued)

	1964			1966			1970		
	Con	Lab	Oth	Con	Lab	Oth	Con	Lab	Oth
Private/service college	–	–	–	–	–	–	3	–	–
Private/university	1	–	–	–	–	–	1	–	–
Private/service/univ.	1	–	–	–	–	1	1	–	–
Private/professional	–	–	–	–	–	–	–	–	–
Public only	10	3	–	3	–	–	15	–	–
Public/professional	5	1	–	1	–	–	5	1	–
Public/service college	1	–	–	–	–	–	3	–	–
Public/'Oxbridge'	32	12	1	6	6	2	31	6	–
Public/other university	5	5	1	1	5	2	7	1	–
Foreign/UK university	–	–	–	–	–	–	–	1	–
Abroad	–	–	–	–	–	–	–	–	–
INA	–	–	–	–	–	–	1	–	–
Total	64	106	6	13	72	5	92	64	4
All public schools	53	21	2	11	11	–	61	8	–
Eton	14	1	–	2	1	–	11	–	–
Oxford	18	10	1	2	9	–	19	8	–
Cambridge	18	9	–	4	8	3	18	4	–
London	1	8	–	1	12	–	8	6	–
Wales	–	3	1	–	3	–	1	6	–
Scotland	1	5	2	–	4	1	–	5	–
Ireland	1	–	–	–	–	–	1	–	1
Foreign	–	1	–	–	1	–	–	–	–
Other universities	6	12	–	1	9	1	5	7	–
All universities	45	48	4	8	46	5	52	36	1

	Feb. 1974			Oct. 1974		
	Con	Lab	Oth	Con	Lab	Oth
Elementary only	–	4	–	–	–	–
Elementary +	–	2	–	–	–	–
Secondary only	1	6	3	1	3	1
Secondary +	–	8	1	–	1	–
Secondary/professional	1	4	2	–	2	–
Secondary/university	7	19	7	–	11	4
Secondary/service college	–	–	–	–	–	–
Secondary/service/univ.	–	–	–	–	–	–
Private only	–	–	–	–	–	–
Private/service college	–	–	–	–	–	–
Private/university	–	–	–	–	–	–
Private/service/university	–	–	–	–	–	–
Private/professional	–	–	–	–	–	–
Public only	9	–	3	–	–	–
Public/professional	5	–	–	–	–	1
Public/service college	1	–	–	1	–	–
Public/'Oxbridge'	33	3	2	5	2	1
Public/other university	5	–	2	1	2	–
Foreign/UK university	–	–	–	–	1	–

(Table continued on facing page)

Table 4.3 (continued)

	Feb. 1974 Con	Feb. 1974 Lab	Feb. 1974 Oth	Oct. 1974 Con	Oct. 1974 Lab	Oct. 1974 Oth
Abroad	–	–	–	–	–	–
INA	–	–	1	–	–	–
Total	62	46	21	8	22	7
All public schools	54	3	7	7	4	2
Eton	9	–	–	–	–	–
Oxford	16	7	2	2	2	–
Cambridge	21	–	–	3	3	1
London	3	7	–	–	1	–
Wales	1	1	1	–	–	1
Scotland	2	3	6	1	2	3
Ireland	–	–	1	–	–	–
Foreign	1	–	–	–	1	–
Other university	1	5	1	–	7	–
All universities	45	22	11	6	16	5

Since 1970 the Conservative Front Bench has been richer in grammar school MPs, but in this respect the hierarchy of the parliamentary party are ahead of their backbenchers. Constituency selection committees show few signs of moving away from their traditional preference for men of breeding and achievement.

Above all else, the public school has remained the crucial channel of access into the Conservative Party. The 'old school tie' remains the most important qualification available to prospective Conservative MPs, as the success rates of public school candidates indicates. As a guarantee of electoral success, it ranks with the reliability afforded by sponsorship from the mineworkers' union in the Labour Party [7]. Clearly, the better Conservative seats do discriminate in favour of public school candidates, and whilst there might have been some slight lessening in the preponderance of old-Etonian MPs, the overall pre-eminence of the public schools in the parliamentary ranks of the Conservative Party has been immutable (Table 4.4).

Just under half of all MPs (46·7 per cent) at these ten elections were recruited from the public schools. By contrast, approximately four per cent of schoolchildren attend such a school. Among Conservative MPs, the proportion exceeds three quarters (77·8 per cent). It is obviously difficult to overstate the sheer numerical dominance of the public schools in the Conservative Party. Throughout, the public school/Oxbridge route has proven the most popular preparation for a Conservative career in Parliament. This route was followed by 46·7 per cent of Conservatives and a graduate qualification has been the most likely consequence of a public school education. This is hardly surprising, since a primary function of public school education is to secure university admission, and almost invariably at Oxbridge.

Table 4.4

Some major educational backgrounds of Conservative MPs

(a) All Conservatives

	1945	1950	1951	1955	1959	1964	1966	1970	*Feb.* 1974	*Oct.* 1974
Elementary*	0·5	1·0	1·0	1·5	1·4	1·0	1·2	1·2	1·0	1·1
Public/Oxbridge	50·3	51·9	51·0	51·3	46·5	49·3	51·6	44·7	48·3	47·5
Eton	27·1	26·7	23·7	23·1	19·4	22·2	21·8	19·0	18·2	17·0
Public school	83·2	83·1	70·2	79·7	75·8	77·9	78·9	74·2	75·0	74·6
'Oxbridge'	53·3	54·0	54·3	53·7	50.6	54·3	57·1	51·3	55·7	55·1
All universities	64·7	64·7	64·6	64·9	60·7	63·8	67·0	63·5	66·9	67·4

(b) New Conservatives

	Pre- 1945	1945	1950	1951	1955	1959	1964	1966	1970	*Feb.* 1974	*Oct.* 1974
Elementary*	–	1·4	2·0	–	4·5	–	1·5	–	1·1	–	–
Public/Oxbridge	56·3	43·5	44·9	43·8	47·4	39·4	50·0	46·1	34·1	53·2	62·5
Eton	27·8	26·1	21·4	25·0	20·5	16·3	21·9	15·4	12·1	14·5	–
Public school	85·3	81·2	76·5	68·7	70·5	73·1	82·9	84·5	67·0	85·6	87·5
'Oxbridge'	61·4	42·1	46·9	53·1	50·0	45·2	56·3	46·1	40·7	59·7	62·5
All universities	73·4	50·8	61·3	56·3	66·3	53·8	70·4	62·0	57·2	72·6	75·0

* Includes 'elementary plus'

The extent of the preference shown for public school candidates can be seen by their numbers who are successful in times of national defeat for the Conservative Party (Tables 4.4(b) and 4.3). The new Conservatives who are returned in years of national defeat (i.e., those elected in the safer constituencies) contain larger proportions of public school men than at other elections. The 1945, 1964, 1966 and February and October 1974 cohorts are abundant with public school and public school/Oxbridge recruits. There can be little doubt that the better Conservative constituencies retain their affinity for the public schools.

The standing of graduates in this party has always been high and at each of the ten elections between 60 per cent and 68 per cent of Conservative MPs have held graduate qualifications: of these, the overwhelming majority are from Oxford or Cambridge. At each of the ten post-war elections over half of the Conservative Party were Oxbridge recruits and, as with public school men, they too have found some discrimination shown in their favour by the better constituencies.

In terms of educational experiences in the Conservative Party there emerges a clear and relatively unchanging picture of recruitment from narrow and exclusive sources [8]. Although there have been some adjustments at higher levels in the parliamentary party, there has been little, if any, weakening of the preference shown towards the twin attributes of rank and attainment. Those who possess these virtues have found their election easiest and earliest. Moreover, the predominance of public school recruits makes for a much more socially homogeneous party than the Labour Party.

Labour: towards meritocracy [9]

Two distinct features mark the educational backgrounds of Labour MPs in this period. The first is the quite dramatic shift towards better educated Labour representatives (fashionably described as the new meritocracy) and the second,which is affected by this process, is the existence within the PLP of distinct educational groupings. At ministerial levels the two major parties differ less than they do at backbench level. Whilst the Conservative Party has homogeneous educational recruitment, there are very different routes of access into Labour parliamentary politics, and over this period of thirty years, one is rapidly being displaced.

For many Labour MPs the only formal schooling which they received was in an elementary board or council school, which represented the minimum state provision before the 1944 Education Act. Some of these went on later in life to receive technical or adult training, but for most formal education did not stretch beyond an elementary school. Nearly one third of Labour MPs in this period received simply an elementary or elementary plus education. Historically, these men from the grass roots of the Labour movement have played an important part in Labour politics. In the interwar years, they comprised three-quarters of all Labour MPs [10]. The Labour Party acted, in part, as a vehicle to secure the representation of the working classes by their own kind. Since 1945, the displacement of the elementary educated has been both thorough and rapid.

In 1945, 45 per cent of Labour MPs had an elementary education (Table 4.5). By the time Labour assumed office in 1964 this had fallen to 29·7 per cent and by October 1974 it was 16 per cent. Although there is evidence to suggest that the proportion of Labour elementary educated MPs increased when that party lost an election (because they have tended to be adopted in better Labour seats) their steady disappearance from the Labour benches has been a ceaseless process. The explanation for their adoption in better seats can be found quite simply with the trade unions who have frequently favoured the notion of actual representation [11]. But this tendency has itself been subjected to change in recent years.

Naturally, the change in terminology brought about by the 1944 Education Act, when all children began to receive some form of secondary education, and the consequent increase in educational opportunities, could account for the displacement of the elementary educated. For this to be so, however, it would be expected that the decrease in the size of the elementary group would be more or less replaced by the size of the secondary group (i.e., those with a secondary or secondary plus background). This is not the case, and the proportion of Labour MPs with just a secondary school education has been fairly stable at around 13 per cent. What has happened is that there has been an important shift away from the working class. In particular, they have been replaced by the grammar school/university products, who with some intelligence and a little effort, form what has been described as the meritocracy.

Table 4.5
Some major educational backgrounds of Labour MPs

(a) All Labour

	1945	1950	1951	1955	1959	1964	1966	1970	Feb. 1974	Oct. 1974
Elementary*	43·0	41·2	39·4	37·8	35·9	29·7	25·6	22·1	18·6	16·0
Secondary/university	18·7	18·6	18·8	18·6	20·3	24·6	29·8	35·0	39·0	40·3
Public/Oxbridge	10·4	12·5	13·7	13·1	12·9	12·9	12·7	12·8	9·7	10·4
Public school	19·4	22·2	23·4	23·5	24·6	24·0	22·8	19·4	15·7	16·4
Oxbridge	14·5	15·4	16·8	16·4	17·2	17·7	19·3	20·4	19·3	20·8
London	6·5	5·5	4·8	7·3	8·2	9·1	9·9	11·7	11·3	11·0
All universities	34·2	37·7	38·7	38·2	39·5	43·9	48·5	51·2	53·0	55·7

(b) New Labour

	Pre-1945	1945	1950	1951	1955	1959	1964	1966	1970	Feb. 1974	Oct. 1974
Elementary*	49·3	38·0	33·8	20·0	26·9	45·3	25·5	13·9	12·5	13·0	–
Secondary/univ.	17·5	19·4	19·4	26·7	26·9	26·2	29·2	48·6	43·7	41·3	50·0
Public/Oxbridge	9·8	12·2	16·1	6·7	7·7	2·4	11·3	8·3	9·4	6·5	9·1
Public school	18·2	21·5	27·4	13·3	15·4	11·9	19·8	15·3	12·5	6·5	18·2
Oxbridge	11·7	17·7	19·4	13·3	7·7	4·8	17·9	23·6	18·8	15·2	22·7
London	5·2	7·2	6·4	–	19·2	16·7	7·5	16·7	9·4	15·2	4·5
All universities	30·5	37·6	43·6	40·0	34·6	31·0	45·3	63·9	56·2	47·8	72·7

* Includes 'elementary plus'

For some years, and especially in the sixties, there has been a concern to raise the ability of Labour recruits. Labour's leadership, which has long been middle class, has been especially vocal in pursuit of this end. The sentiments were simply expressed in the words of a young Fabian: 'With all the education there is about these days Labour must show that its candidates are as well qualified as the Tories' [12]. It is one way of establishing that Labour is 'fit to govern', a message which the Labour Party has been concerned to get across to the wider electorate since 1945. This emphasis on ability places a premium on educational qualification and fluency of speech and ideas.

The non-sponsored Labour seats were the first to be attracted to the meritocracy, and the process of embourgeoisement in these constituencies has been that much more rapid. But the trade union seats have also been penetrated by these younger and better educationally qualified candidates.

The consequence of this change in recruitment is the replacement of those who received only a basic education by new secondary school/university products. Indeed, this replacement is so neat that the figures almost exactly correspond (Figure 4.1). In 1945, 43 per cent of the PLP were elementary educated and 18·7 per cent had attended a secondary school followed by university. By October 1974, 16 per cent were elementary educated and 40·3 per cent were secondary school graduates.

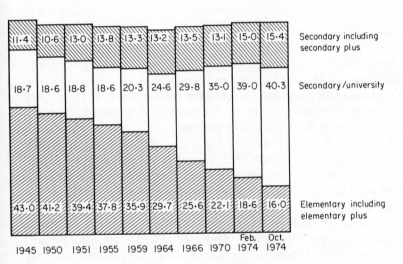

Figure 4.1   Some major Labour educational backgrounds (percentages)

The group receiving a secondary or secondary plus education has been stable, and to take account of all the meritocrats it would really be appropriate to combine the secondary/professional group with the secondary/university group. This process is reflected in the growing number of Labour graduates. In 1945, 43·2 per cent of Labour MPs were graduates. The 1970 cohort was the first to contain a majority of graduates and by October 1974 the figure had risen to 55·7 per cent.

In one further important respect, the Labour Party does not resemble the Conservative Party. In the Labour Party, the public schools are a much less important factor in recruitment. Whilst nearly 80 per cent of Conservatives attended a public school. more than 80 per cent of Labour MPs did not, although at 18·7 per cent, the proportion of public school men in the Labour Party might be considered unduly high and, if measured in terms of ministerial positions, this figure would be even higher. Important Labour figures, of both Right and Left, have been public school products, but they remain a minority of Labour MPs and there is evidence to indicate that they certainly do not enjoy tenure in the better seats, unlike their Conservative counterparts.

In educational terms, then, the pattern of Labour recruitment over these thirty years is primarily coloured by this shift from the workers to the able and articulate. It is a pattern which is repeated in occupational terms, and as with Labour occupations, there are distinct groupings. Unlike the homogeneous character of the Conservative Party, there is diversity in Labour MPs' educational origins which range from elementary through grammar school/university to public school/-Oxbridge.

Minor parties

It is a rather unsatisfactory, and possibly misleading, exercise to aggregate the educational backgrounds of the various groups which comprise the minor parties. The overall picture falls somewhere between the predominant Conservative and Labour images, but it includes a range which extends from the elementary educated to the best traditions of the Conservative patricians.

At the lower end of the scale of formal educational attainment are the collection of Ulster MPs who have been elected, under various banners, during the post-war years. They most closely resemble the working class representatives of the Labour Party. Next come the United Ulster Unionists who emerge as a new party after the February 1974 elections, with four of their number who are graduates. Of all groups the Nationalists exhibit most educational attainment, and all but one of this group possess university degrees. If they are compared to the major parties they closely resemble the Labour meritocracy. For the most part their elevation to the political élite has followed the secondary school/university route, although the presence of the SNP and PLC parties does have the particular effect of strengthening the representation of the Scottish and Welsh Universities at Westminster. With the Liberals there is a virtual reproduction of Conservative educational profiles. The public schools and universities of Oxford and Cambridge are much in evidence, and the only major difference seems to be that in the range of public schools attended the prestigious public schools are much less predominant. Thus, whatever else they may bring into parliamentary politics, the minor parties do not bring radically different social pedigrees.

Converging parties

In describing the patterns of political recruitment in educational terms over these thirty years, it is tempting to elevate the data into some kind of thesis about the converging nature of the two main British political parties. Superficially, at least, there would appear considerable evidence to support such an interpretation.

Certainly, there has been a continuing process of embourgeoisement in the Parliamentary Labour Party and the rump of the 'pure' working class representatives has suffered continuing depletion with consecutive general elections. Even the trade unions, who have customarily had the greatest affinity with the workers, have increasingly looked outside their own rank and file when selecting parliamentary candidates. In crude terms, the intellectuals have replaced the practitioners. On the Conservative side there has been additional evidence afforded to the thesis by the lesser drift away from the traditional patrician class, at the higher levels, if not at backbench level. The result is to cement the foundations of both the two major parliamentary parties firmly in the professional middle class. But to leave it at this, to settle for a semblance of overlap and convergence would be both shallow and misleading. There remain crucial differences between these two parties.

One essential difference in the educational profiles of the Conservative and Labour Parties is obscured by the crude manner in which the appropriate demographic data is assembled. The aggregate statistics tell us something about the opportunities for political recruitment from certain institutions and also about the direction of change during these thirty years, but they fail to record or examine the nature of the effort which was required in order to achieve that education. A public school education is fairly indicative of social status if only because of the financial exclusiveness of such schools, but a degree may be the natural product of a middle class education or the culmination of a protracted struggle through the state school system. Despite all the attempts to widen university entries, the proportion of working class children receiving the benefit of a university education has not changed greatly since the 1930s [13]. Thus, whilst the actual universities or even schools attended might be the same, the effort required in order to achieve this level of education might vary considerably. It is an important distinction both in differentiating the parties and also in understanding the effect of educational training and backgrounds upon attitude formation. The notion of meritocracy is, of course, intended to meet this methodological problem and reflect effort as well as attainment.

A second, crucial, distinction is more apparent within the data itself. It is easy in looking at channels of political recruitment to concentrate upon the general and blur the particular. Thus, it might seem appropriate to deduce from the aggregate data that there is now an approximate equivalence in the recruitment of Conservative and Labour graduates. But the particular channels through which recruitment operates are, in understanding both opportunities and attitudes, probably much more important than general educational backgrounds. Actual pathways to the Commons are more important than the wider routes. The majority of Conservative graduates are Oxbridge; the majority of Labour graduates are not. Similarly, not only is there a considerable and vital disparity in the numbers from the two major parties drawn from the public schools, the actual range of public schools attended varies between parties. Some sense of this can be achieved by examining the productivity of particular educational sources of parliamentary recruits.

Table 4.6
Leading public schools

	No.	%
Eton	174	21·7
Harrow	43	5·4
Winchester	29	3·6
		30·7
Charterhouse	19	
Westminster	19	
Cheltenham	18	
Haileybury	17	
Marlborough	17	
Rugby	16	
Wellington	15	
Repton	13	
Fettes	11	
Uppingham	9	
Stowe	8	
Clifton	6	
Whitgift	6	
	420	52·3
Others	383	47·7
Total	803	100·0

The public schools are, of course, the most obvious route to Westminster and nearly one half of MPs come through this channel. To probe a little deeper, however, reveals a distinct élite even within these institutions. Of those MPs drawn from the public schools, 21·7 per cent attended just one school — Eton (Table 4.6). 'To be an Etonian', wrote Christopher Hollis, with some justification, 'is in itself a real social distinction'. One is reminded of how Gladstone's biographer, Philip Magnus, describes the future Prime Minister at Eton, 'inscribing and preserving a number of envelopes in copper-plate handwriting: The Right Honourable W.E. Gladstone, M.P.' [14]. Certain institutions not only provide access to the political élite, but plainly propogate the values and motivations necessary to seek elevation to that élite. Whilst Eton's supremacy in this field has been unrivalled, there is a clear order of rank among the public schools: 30·7 per cent of public school men attended one of three schools and over half are from what might be described as the 'Top Sixteen'. However, if we separate Conservative and Labour public school recruits, there is a notable distinction. Of the 619 public school Conservatives, 165 went to Eton and 218 to one of the top three schools – over one quarter of the party attended one of three schools. Of the equivalent 154 Labour MPs, only 8 attended Eton and 14 one of the top three schools. Therefore, not only are Labour recruits much less likely to have attended public school, but those that did were not filtered through the same narrow and particular public school channel as the public school Conservatives.

A similar pattern emerges in the range of universities attended (Table 4.7): 909 MPs followed a university degree course and just three, admittedly the largest – Oxford, Cambridge and London – account for nearly three-quarters of these graduates. As with the public schools, there is a rank order of universities, and again if we separate the parties, there is a distinction to be made. 86 per cent of Conservative graduates hold an Oxbridge degree whilst of Labour graduates, 38 per cent come from Oxbridge, although even this figure exaggerates the proportion of the student population attending these two universities.

Table 4.7
Leading universities

	Con.	Labour	Other	Total	%
Oxford	255	90	11	326	35·9
Cambridge	180	47	8	235	25·9
London	24	75	1	100	11·0
					72·8
Wales	5	25	7	37	
Scotland	19	43	14	76	
Ireland	11	3	2	16	
Foreign	9	7	–	16	
Manchester	6	20	3	29	
Liverpool	2	11	1	14	
Leeds	4	9	–	13	
Birmingham	5	6	–	11	
Durham	4	5	–	9	
Southampton	1	8	–	9	
Sheffield	2	3	–	5	
Others	6	6	–	12	
Total	503	359	47	909	

Even at the level of Oxbridge colleges there is an indication of rank (Table 4.8). Four Oxford Colleges – Christ Church, Balliol, New and Magdalen – account for

56·1 per cent of Oxford educated MPs. Similarly, four Cambridge Colleges — Trinity, Trinity Hall, Kings and Gonville and Caius — are equally politically prolific, producing 53·2 per cent of Cambridge MPs. (Indeed, Trinity alone can claim 26·4 per cent of the Cambridge group). Again, as with the range of public schools and universities, exclusiveness is much more apparent in the Conservative ranks than it is in the Labour Party.

Table 4.8
Leading Oxbridge colleges

Oxford				*Cambridge*		
	No.	%			No.	%
Christ Church	55	16·9	Trinity		62	26·4
Balliol	51	15·6	Trinity Hall		25	10·6
New	41	12·6	Kings		20	8·5
Magdalen	36	11·0	Gonville & Caius		18	7·7
	183	56·1			125	53·2
Others	143	43·9	Others		110	46·8
Total	326	100·0	Total		235	100·0

This brief review of the particular educational paths taken by political recruits gives some indication that there remain crucial differences in the socio-economic composition of the two major parliamentary parties. Certainly, the educational backgrounds of Labour MPs have changed considerably over the past three decades, and there was a notable acceleration of this process in the sixties. But even the interpretation of this dramatic change has to be treated with some caution. A university education does not in itself necessarily imply automatic transfer to middle class status and values. A recent survey of graduates has shown how, even after obtaining a degree, a working class student's 'attitudes and aspirations are likely still to be heavily influenced by his social background' [15]. The universities are not quite the 'melting pot' they are sometimes taken to be and, as may be seen in the choice of professions which Labour graduates select, there remain vital dissimilarities in the nature of professional groups among Conservative and Labour parties. That the PLP has adopted novel channels of recruitment is clear, but to deduce from this a growing convergence between the parties is much less clear. Above all the Conservative Party retains its essential homogeneity whilst Labour continues to have a much more diverse profile.

Notes

[1]   By classifying, for example, parental occupations.
[2]   W.L. Guttsman, 'Elite Recruitment and Political Leadership in Britain and

Germany since 1950: a Comparative Study of MPs and Cabinets', in I. Crewe (ed.), *British Political Sociology Yearbook*, vol. 1, Croom Helm, London, 1974, p. 101.

[3] See, for example, T. May, 'A Government of Meritocrats', *New Society*, 12 May 1977.

[4] See, more fully, the discussion of methodology in Ch. 1.

[5] R. Rose, *The Problem of Party Government*, Macmillan, London, 1975, p.54.

[6] Although, of course, both went on to Oxford, and Mrs Thatcher's victory brought into Conservative Central Office some more 'traditional' Conservatives.

[7] See Chapter 7. The percentage success rates of candidates with certain major educational backgrounds are:

Conservative

	1951	1955	1959	1964	1966	1970	Feb. 1974	Oct. 1974
'Oxbridge'	84	73	70	61	55	68	67	65
Public school	65	67	69	54	49	66	60	54
Eton	79	80	81	72	65	86	76	65

Labour

	1951	1955	1959	1964	1966	1970	Feb. 1974	Oct. 1974
Elementary	63	60	61	71	81	79	79	72
University	47	44	42	49	58	45	45	49

[8] See below, pp. 53–6.

[9] M. Young, *The Rise of the Meritocracy*, Penguin, London, 1961.

[10] W.L. Guttsman, *The British Political Elite*, MacGibbon and Kee, London, 1968, p. 105.

[11] Representation by their own men. See Chapter 7.

[12] B. Lapping and G. Roddice (eds), *More Power to the People: Young Fabian Essays on Democracy in Britain*, Longman, London, 1968, pp. 25–6.

[13] R.K. Kelsall, A. Poole and A. Kuhn, *Graduates: The Sociology of An Elite*, Methuen, London, 1972. This observation refers to the period when current MPs would have graduated.

[14] P. Magnus, *Gladstone*, Murray, London, 1954, p. 8.

[15] R.K. Kelsall, et al. 'University – a chance to succeed?', *Times Higher Education Supplement*, 25 February 1972.

5 The occupational background of MPs

The range of occupations in which Members were engaged prior to their election to Parliament naturally reflects the main features and trends of their educational profiles. In the Conservative Party there is again a picture of homogeneity and exclusiveness, with over half of their MPs drawn from just three occupations – barristers, directors and farmers. Labour Members are drawn from more diverse backgrounds stretching from the unskilled manual workers to the established professions of law and medicine. But this diversity in occupational background in no way disguises the quite dramatic expansion of the professions in the PLP at the direct expense of the manual workers. The embourgeoisement of the Labour Party over these three decades can be expressed in sharp relief by examining the changing occupational backgrounds of Labour parliamentary recruits.

Introduction

The profession of politics places peculiar demands upon those who opt for public life. Robert Louis Stevenson wrote that 'Politics is perhaps the only profession for which no preparation is thought necessary'. But the reality is that a career in Parliament appeals to people of a certain type. Political life calls for fluency of mind and speech, ambition, some administrative and managerial skills and, frequently, opportunism. The profession of politics not surprisingly attracts the 'communicating' professions – lawyers, lecturers, teachers and journalists – and such professions dominate not just the British legislature but most parliamentary democracies.

The nature of employment is also important because some, more easily than others, allow for the time that is necessary in order to achieve and retain candidatures. A century ago Parliament was dominated by aristocratic and landed gentry, who had the financial resources and leisure to indulge in political life. Their places have been taken by members of the professions. The gentleman farmer has replaced the aristocrat and the director has replaced the rentier. Ivor Jennings has suggested that 'in an age when almost everybody has to earn his living' Members are likely to be drawn from certain occupations which are compatible with the demands of a parliamentary career [1]. He gives the examples of the London professional man who can devote the morning to his own career, the retired serviceman, trade union officials who are able to find 'administrative or advisory appointments in London', and journalists and broadcasters who are able with ease to supplement their parliamentary salary. The rising fortune of the teaching profession as a source of political recruitment is, therefore, rather notable since it less easily lends itself to supplementary employment, at least for the duration of their stay at Westminster.

This correlation between certain professions and inclination to stand for public office is not unique to Britain as virtually the same range of occupations dominate most other legislatures. Ross, for example, has commented that 'a glut of lawyers seems to afflict legislative bodies generally', [2] and indeed, high as the British figure is, lawyers are even more plentiful in other legislatures. Between 1945 and 1974, the proportion of British lawyer MPs (including barristers and solicitors) stands at 15·6 per cent. Comparable figures for other legislatures include: United States, 55 per cent; Brazil, 50 per cent; France, 32 per cent; Italy 27 per cent, and Germany, 19 per cent. It is not too difficult to understand the attraction of making the laws for those who normally practice the law. But the regularity of some occupations in providing political recruits extends beyond the legal profession. The most recent major review of political recruitment analysed 1,548 Brazilian Federal Deputies in the period 1945–75, and the author of that study noted that: 'The most frequent principal occupations observed were practising lawyers, teachers, doctors, public functionaries, agriculture and journalists. In terms of multiple occupations, lawyers, teachers and journalists were most frequent' [3]. With the exception of the business group in the Conservative Party and the rump of manual workers in the Labour Party, an almost identical description could be applied to legislative recruitment in Britain during the same thirty years.

Occupation, like education, is difficult to classify and all that can be achieved is, at best, an approximation of reality. Multiple occupations are especially problematic and many MPs list two or three occupations. Rather than record several occupations against a Member, some selection has been exercised in order to identify formative or principal occupation. Naturally this will be an arbitrary choice on occasions but, since regular criteria have been used in making this choice, it should prove reasonably consistent. One particular effect of this is to define the professions of law and journalism with rigour and only allow this classification to stand where a Member is principally and actively engaged in such a field.

As with education, the data is recorded on an augmented version of the Nuffield schedule, the main alteration being the refinement of some categories in the professional, business and miscellaneous sections [4]. An important addition is the inclusion of trade union officials in this latter section. Since the primary concern is with principal occupation, it would seem misleading to include under 'workers' a Member who, in fact, was only actively engaged in manual work for a few years and spent the majority of his pre-parliamentary career occupying a white-collar position in a trade union. There is a difference between those who actually perform manual work and those who concern themselves with workers' remuneration and conditions of employment. The majority of officials have been previously engaged in manual work, but this is not invariably the case as it is not unknown for trade union officials (usually the white-collar unions) to have public school backgrounds. For these reasons, manual workers and trade union officials have been separated and the latter included in the miscellaneous section. One incidental result of this is to make even steeper the marked decline in Labour worker representatives [5] .

Conservatives: law, land and business

In their occupational backgrounds Conservatives during these three decades have retained their essential cohesiveness and symmetry. There has been some sedate movement away from the landed (defined here, somewhat conservatively, as farmers) to the benefit of business, described by one Conservative MP in cricketing terms as a change from 'gentlemen' to 'players' [6] , but in comparison with Labour the Conservative Party changes are subtle. In 1945, 61·4 per cent of the Conservative Party were recruited from the ranks of barristers, directors and farmers:, in October 1974 the three occupations accounted for 55 per cent of Conservatives at Westminster. The description which Blondel has applied to the Conservatives has remained valid throughout this period: ' . . . an organic union of all the groups composing the middle classes, not a juxtaposition of separate elements. It is a result which few parties of the Right have been able to achieve in other countries' [7] .

Over these ten elections more than four-fifths of Conservative MPs have been drawn from professional and business occupations. They, together with farming and occasionally journalism, are the normal and almost exclusive access route to the Conservative Party in Parliament (Figure 5.1). Despite their vital contribution to the Conservative vote, and periodic claims about Conservative concern for the rank and file trade unionists and shop floor workers, the constituency parties have proven almost wholly impervious to Central Office protestations to allow Conservative workers to reach the Commons. It was only possible to identify one worker Tory in the Commons during the whole of this period (Table 5.1). (This excludes spasmodic white collar trade unionists and young men working their way quickly up the family business.)

Of all professions, barristers have consistently provided the largest number of Conservative recruits: at any election, the proportion of Conservative lawyers has fluctuated within the narrow range of 15·4 per cent to 19·6 per cent. And not only do they outnumber their counterparts in the Labour Party, those who were engaged in legal practice on this side of the House generally attain a higher level of distinction in their calling [8] . This, of course, supports Rush's observation that many Conservative Associations maintain the requirement that candidates 'should have proved themselves in some sphere other than politics' [9] . Furthermore, there is some evidence, although slight, that barristers are more likely to appear in the better Conservative seats (Tables 5.2 and 5.3 and later abstracted in Figure 5.3).

The other professions reasonably well represented on the Conservative benches are the armed forces and diplomatic services. The contribution of the armed forces to Conservative political recruitment is further explored in Chapter 7, suffice it to say here that over the period as a whole, commissioned servicemen have figured quite prominently in the Conservative Party, but if we examine their recruitment by successive cohorts, their declining importance is apparent (Table 5.3) [10]. In the last four intakes of new Conservatives, only four regular servicemen appear.

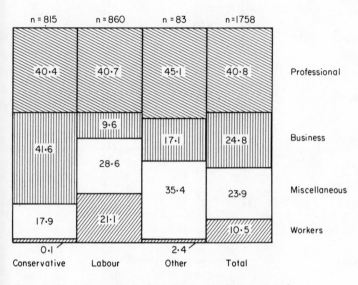

Figure 5.1   Occupational backgrounds (percentages)

Table 5.1
Occupations of all MPs, 1945–1974

	Con	Lab	Oth	Total	per cent
Barrister	135	65	8	208	(12·0)
Solicitor	25	32	5	62	
Chartered surveyor/engineer	17	24	3	44	
Civil service/local government	5	13	–	18	
Services	59	3	–	62	
Diplomatic services	28	3	1	32	
Lecturer	8	91	5	104	(11·1)
School teacher	10	71	7	88	
Doctor/dentist	11	19	3	33	
Chartered accountant/secretary	21	9	3	33	
Scientific worker	1	7	–	8	
Minister of religion	2	5	2	9	
Social worker	4	3	–	7	
Total (professions)	326	345	37	708	40·8

(Table continued overleaf)

Table 5.1 (continued)

	Con	Lab	Oth	Total	per cent
Small business	2	7	2	11	
Director	245	21	7	273	(15·7)
Banker/financier	18	1	–	19	
Executive/management	23	28	–	51	
Commerce/insurance	34	3	2	39	
Business consultant	13	10	3	26	
Clerical	1	11	–	12	
Total (business)	336	81	14	431	24·8
White collar	2	35	2	39	
Political worker	9	13	1	23	
Trade union official	–	98	–	98	(5·6)
Farmer/landowner	82	7	15	104	(6·0)
Housewife	3	7	–	10	
Student	5	–	1	6	
Journalist/author	34	69	10	113	(6·5)
Public relations	8	11	–	19	
Actor	–	1	–	1	
Pilot	1	–	–	1	
Policeman	–	1	–	1	
Total (miscellaneous)	144	242	29	415	23·9
Railwayman	–	35	–	35	
Miner	–	62	–	62	
Skilled worker	1	53	1	55	
Semi/unskilled worker	–	29	1	30	
Total (workers)	1	179	2	182	10·5
INA	8	13	1	22	
Grand total	815	860	83	1758	

Table 5.2
Occupations of all MPs, by election

	1945			1950			1951		
	Con	Lab	Oth	Con	Lab	Oth	Con	Lab	Oth
Barrister	37	34	4	51	34	5	55	29	5
Solicitor	4	12	1	10	12	2	11	10	1
Ch. surveyor/engineer	3	12	2	5	8	–	6	7	–
Civil service/local govt.	3	3	–	2	3	–	2	2	–
Services	30	3	–	30	1	–	31	1	–
Diplomatic services	8	1	1	11	2	–	12	?	–
Lecturer	5	20	33	4	19	–	5	19	–
School teacher	1	27	–	–	24	–	–	24	–
Doctor/dentist	2	11	2	4	8	–	4	8	–

(Table continued on facing page)

Table 5.2 (continued)

	1945 Con	Lab	Oth	1950 Con	Lab	Oth	1951 Con	Lab	Oth
Ch.accountant/secretary	4	5	–	5	3	–	5	2	–
Scientific worker	–	2	–	1	1	–	1	1	–
Minister of religion	1	4	–	1	3	–	–	2	–
Social worker	1	–	–	1	–	–	2	–	–
Total (professions)	99	134	13	125	118	7	134	107	6
Small business	–	3	–	–	2	–	–	2	–
Director	67	11	1	100	8	1	109	9	–
Banker/financier	1	1	–	4	–	–	2	–	–
Executive/management	2	7	–	6	4	–	6	3	–
Commerce/insurance	7	1	–	8	2	–	10	2	1
Business consultant	–	3	1	–	4	–	–	3	–
Clerical	–	5	–	–	3	–	–	3	–
Total (business)	77	31	2	118	23	1	127	22	1
White collar	–	13	–	–	11	1	–	10	1
Political worker	1	3	1	4	3	–	4	3	–
Trade union official	–	50	–	–	36	–	–	36	–
Farmer/landowner	25	5	5	28	2	2	32	1	2
Housewife	–	3	–	–	3	–	–	2	–
Student	3	–	–	4	–	–	3	–	–
Journalist/author	5	38	5	13	30	2	13	32	–
Public relations	–	2	–	1	1	–	1	1	–
Actor	–	–	–	–	–	–	–	–	–
Pilot	–	–	–	–	–	–	–	–	–
Policeman	–	1	–	–	–	–	–	–	–
Total (miscellaneous)	34	115	11	50	86	5	53	85	3
Railwayman	–	27	–	–	18	–	–	18	–
Miner	–	39	–	–	32	–	–	28	–
Skilled worker	–	27	1	–	20	–	–	19	–
Semi/unskilled worker	–	14	–	–	13	–	–	11	–
Total (workers)	0	107	1	0	83	0	0	76	0
INA	3	13	0	4	5	0	6	5	0
Grand total	213	400	27	297	315	13	320	295	10

	1955 Con	Lab	Oth	1959 Con	Lab	Oth	1964 Con	Lab	Oth
Barrister	60	28	5	66	25	4	58	27	4
Solicitor	11	9	1	12	9	1	13	14	–
Ch. surveyor/engineer	6	8	–	8	7	–	6	13	–
Civil service/local govt.	1	2·	–	1	4	–	–	5	–
Services	36	1	–	30	1	–	20	1	–
Diplomatic services	14	2	–	14	2	–	17	1	–
Lecturer	3	13	–	3	17	–	3	24	–

(Table continued overleaf)

Table 5.2 (continued)

	1955			1959			1964		
	Con	Lab	Oth	Con	Lab	Oth	Con	Lab	Oth
School teacher	1	26	–	2	21	–	2	28	1
Doctor/dentist	5	7	–	5	6	–	3	7	–
Ch.accountant/secretary	5	2	–	8	3	–	6	5	–
Scientific worker	1	1	–	–	2	–	–	2	–
Minister of religion	–	2	–	–	2	–	–	2	–
Social worker	4	–	–	2	–	–	2	–	–
Total (professions)	147	101	6	151	99	5	130	129	5
Small business	–	2	–	–	2	–	–	2	–
Director	113	10	–	122	6	–	85	6	1
Banker/financier	2	–	–	3	–	–	3	–	–
Executive/management	6	1	–	4	2	–	4	11	–
Commerce/insurance	14	1	1	17	1	1	13	2	–
Business consultant	1	2	–	4	2	–	3	5	1
Clerical	–	3	–	–	4	–	–	5	–
Total (business)	136	19	1	150	17	1	108	31	2
White collar	1	11	1	–	9	–	1	10	–
Political worker	4	4	–	3	4	–	3	5	–
Trade union official	–	32	–	–	39	–	–	37	–
Farmer/landowner	30	2	1	36	3	1	36	4	2
Housewife	1	3	–	1	3	–	–	3	–
Student	3	–	–	1	–	–	1	–	–
Journalist/author	11	29	–	13	26	–	13	35	–
Public relations	2	2	–	2	1	–	3	4	–
Actor	–	–	–	–	–	–	–	–	–
Pilot	–	–	–	–	–	–	–	–	–
Policeman	–	–	–	–	–	–	–	–	–
Total (miscellaneous)	52	81	2	56	85	1	57	98	2
Railwayman	–	16	–	–	9	–	–	10	–
Miner	–	27	–	–	25	–	–	22	–
Skilled worker	1	17	–	1	13	–	1	18	–
Semi/unskilled worker	–	9	1	–	7	–	–	8	–
Total (workers)	1	69	1	1	54	0	1	58	0
INA	7	5	0	7	3	0	5	4	0
Grand total	343	277	10	365	258	7	301	320	9

	1966			1970			Feb. 1974		
	Con	Lab	Oth	Con	Lab	Oth	Con	Lab	Oth
Barrister	48	33	3	50	33	3	50	27	6
Solicitor	13	18	–	13	12	–	11	10	3
Ch.surveyor/engineer	4	13	–	7	11	–	6	10	–
Civil service/local govt.	–	4	–	–	3	–	1	3	–
Services	11	1	–	12	–	–	4	–	–
Diplomatic services	14	1	–	12	1	–	11	1	–

(Table continued on facing page)

Table 5.2 (continued)

	1966 Con	1966 Lab	1966 Oth	1970 Con	1970 Lab	1970 Oth	Feb. 1974 Con	Feb. 1974 Lab	Feb. 1974 Oth
Lecturer	1	43	–	3	36	–	1	43	2
School teacher	1	30	1	7	27	2	5	34	3
Doctor/dentist	2	8	1	6	6	–	3	6	1
Ch.accountant/secretary	6	5	1	7	5	–	9	5	3
Scientific worker	–	2	–	–	3	–	–	4	–
Minister of religion	–	–	–	–	–	1	–	–	2
Social worker	1	1	–	1	1	–	–	1	–
Total (professions)	101	159	6	118	138	6	101	144	20
Small business	–	2	–	2	2	–	1	3	2
Director	74	7	1	94	2	1	83	3	4
Banker/financier	4	–	–	7	–	–	13	–	–
Executive/management	5	14	–	11	10	–	12	12	–
Commerce/insurance	9	2	–	13	1	–	11	1	–
Business consultant	2	6	2	7	6	1	11	6	1
Clerical	–	5	–	1	6	–	–	7	–
Total (business)	94	36	3	135	27	2	131	32	7
White collar	1	14	–	1	14	–	–	15	–
Political worker	2	5	–	3	4	–	5	6	–
Trade union official	–	37	–	–	35	–	–	32	1
Farmer/landowner	34	4	2	35	2	–	28	1	5
Housewife	–	4	–	1	2	–	1	2	–
Student	1	–	–	1	–	1	–	–	–
Journalist/author	13	38	1	21	24	1	20	25	3
Public relations	3	5	–	7	3	–	5	4	–
Actor	–	1	–	–	1	–	–	1	–
Pilot	–	–	–	1	–	–	1	–	–
Policeman	–	–	–	–	–	–	–	–	–
Total (miscellaneous)	54	108	3	70	85	2	60	86	9
Railwayman	–	8	–	–	4	–	–	3	–
Miner	–	22	–	–	14	–	–	10	–
Skilled worker	1	19	–	1	15	–	1	19	1
Semi/unskilled worker	–	11	–	–	5	–	–	5	–
Total (workers)	1	60	0	1	38	0	1	37	1
INA	3	2	0	6	2	0	4	2	0
Grand total	253	365	12	330	290	10	297	301	37

(Table continued overleaf)

Table 5.2 (continued)

	Oct. 1974 Con	Lab	Oth
Barrister	47	28	5
Solicitor	9	10	3
Ch.surveyor/engineer	6	10	1
Civil service/local govt.	1	5	–
Services	4	–	–
Diplomatic services	8	1	–
Lecturer	3	52	2
School teacher	6	37	6
Doctor/dentist	3	6	–
Ch.accountant/secretary	9	5	2
Scientific worker	–	4	–
Minister of religion	–	–	2
Social worker	–	3	–
Total (professions)	96	161	21
Small business	–	3	2
Director	81	3	6
Banker/financier	13	–	–
Executive/management	13	12	–
Commerce/insurance	9	1	–
Business consultant	10	6	1
Clerical	–	7	–
Total (business)	126	32	9
White collar	–	16	–
Political worker	5	8	–
Trade union official	–	31	–
Farmer/landower	22	–	5
Housewife	–	2	–
Student	–	–	–
Journalist/author	17	25	3
Public relations	5	3	–
Actor	–	1	–
Pilot	1	–	–
Policeman	–	–	–
Total (miscellaneous)	50	86	8
Railwayman	–	3	–
Miner	–	10	–
Skilled worker	1	22	1
Semi/unskilled worker)	–	3	–
Total (workers)	1	38	1
INA	4	2	0
Grand total	277	319	39

Table 5.3
Occupations of new MPs, by election

	Pre-1945			1945			1950		
	Con	Lab	Oth	Con	Lab	Oth	Con	Lab	Oth
Barrister	37	13	3	8	24	1	13	6	2
Solicitor	2	6	–	2	6	1	7	4	1
Ch.surveyor/engineer	4	4	2	1	8	–	1	1	–
Civil service/local govt.	3	1	–	–	2	–	–	2	–
Services	18	1	–	15	2	–	4	–	–
Diplomatic services	8	1	1	2	–	–	2	1	–
Lecturer	5	6	2	–	14	1	1	3	–
School teacher	1	9	–	–	18	–	–	8	–
Doctor/dentist	2	6	1	1	5	1	2	1	–
Ch.accountant/secretary	3	4	–	1	5	–	1	–	–
Scientific worker	–	–	–	–	2	–	1	–	–
Minister of religion	1	–	–	–	–	–	1	–	–
Social worker	2	–	–	–	–	–	–	–	–
Total (professions)	86	51	9	30	86	4	33	26	3
Small business	–	1	–	–	2	–	–	–	–
Director	53	4	–	27	8	1	41	1	1
Banker/financier	1	1	–	1	–	–	2	–	–
Executive/management	1	–	–	1	7	–	4	2	–
Commerce/insurance	6	–	–	1	1	–	5	1	–
Business consultant	1	–	1	–	3	–	–	1	–
Clerical	–	1	–	–	4	–	–	–	–
Total (business)	62	7	1	30	25	1	52	5	1
White collar	–	2	1	–	11	–	–	3	–
Political worker	2	1	–	–	2	1	2	–	–
Trade union official	–	14	–	–	36	–	–	10	–
Farmer/landower	19	1	3	10	4	2	7	–	–
Housewife	–	1	–	–	2	–	–	1	–
Student	3	–	–	1	–	–	–	–	–
Journalist/author	6	15	5	2	24	1	6	6	1
Public relations	–	–	–	–	2	–	1	–	–
Actor	–	–	–	–	–	–	–	–	–
Pilot	–	–	–	–	–	–	–	–	–
Policeman	–	1	–	–	–	–	–	–	–
Total (miscellaneous)	30	35	9	13	81	4	16	20	1
Railwayman	–	8	–	–	18	–	–	2	–
Miner	–	30	–	–	10	–	–	3	–
Skilled worker	–	13	1	–	14	–	–	1	–
Semi/unskilled worker	–	9	–	–	5	–	–	5	–
Total (workers)	0	60	1	0	47	0	0	11	0
INA	4	8	1	1	5	0	1	0	0
Grand total	182	161	21	74	244	9	102	62	5

(Table continued overleaf)

Table 5.3 (continued)

	1951 Con	1951 Lab	1951 Oth	1955 Con	1955 Lab	1955 Oth	1959 Con	1959 Lab	1959 Oth
Barrister	9	–	–	16	–	–	18	1	1
Solicitor	2	1	–	1	–	–	4	2	–
Ch.surveyor/engineer	1	1	–	2	1	–	3	–	–
Civil service/local govt.	1	–	–	–	1	–	–	2	–
Services	5	–	–	8	–	–	3	–	–
Diplomatic services	2	–	–	4	–	–	3	–	–
Lecturer	–	–	–	–	2	–	–	4	–
School teacher	–	3	–	1	4	–	1	–	–
Doctor/dentist	–	–	–	1	1	–	1	1	–
Ch.accountant/secretary	–	–	–	2	–	–	4	1	–
Scientific worker	–	–	–	–	–	–	–	1	–
Minister of religion	–	1	–	–	–	–	–	–	–
Social worker	–	–	–	2	–	–	–	–	–
Total (professions)	20	6	0	37	9	0	37	12	1
Small business	–	–	–	–	–	–	–	1	–
Director	9	2	–	19	–	–	31	–	–
Banker/financier	–	–	–	1	–	–	1	–	–
Executive/management	–	–	–	–	1	–	2	2	–
Commerce/insurance	1	–	1	6	–	–	6	–	–
Business consultant	–	–	–	1	–	–	2	1	–
Clerical	–	–	–	–	–	–	–	1	–
Total (business)	10	2	1	27	1	0	42	5	0
White collar	–	–	–	1	1	1	–	1	–
Political worker	–	–	–	–	3	–	1	–	–
Trade union official	–	2	–	–	2	–	–	12	–
Farmer/landowner	5	–	1	8	–	–	17	1	–
Housewife	–	–	–	1	1	–	1	–	–
Student	–	–	–	–	–	–	1	–	–
Journalist/author	1	2	–	1	3	–	4	1	–
Public relations	–	–	–	1	1	–	–	–	–
Actor	–	–	–	–	–	–	–	–	–
Pilot	–	–	–	–	–	–	–	–	–
Policeman	–	–	–	–	–	–	–	–	–
Total (miscellaneous)	6	4	1	12	11	1	24	15	0
Railwayman	–	–	–	–	1	–	–	2	–
Miner	–	1	–	–	3	–	–	5	–
Skilled worker	–	1	–	1	1	–	–	3	–
Semi/unskilled worker	–	1	–	–	–	1	–	–	–
Total (workers)	0	3	0	1	5	1	0	10	0
INA	0	0	0	1	0	0	1	0	0
Grand total	36	15	2	78	26	2	104	42	1

(Table continued on facing page)

Table 5.3 (continued)

	1964			1966			1970		
	Con	Lab	Oth	Con	Lab	Oth	Con	Lab	Oth
Barrister	10	6	1	1	8	–	9	5	–
Solicitor	3	5	–	2	5	–	1	3	–
Ch.surveyor/engineer	2	7	–	–	–	–	3	2	–
Civil service/local govt.	–	1	–	–	–	–	–	1	–
Services	2	–	–	–	–	–	3	–	–
Diplomatic services	5	–	–	–	–	–	–	1	–
Lecturer	–	12	–	–	20	–	2	11	–
School teacher	1	8	1	–	5	–	5	8	1
Doctor/dentist	1	3	–	–	2	1	3	–	–
Ch.accountant/secretary	3	1	–	1	–	1	–	1	–
Scientific worker	–	1	–	–	–	–	–	2	–
Minister of religion	–	–	–	–	–	–	–	–	1
Social worker	–	–	–	–	1	–	–	–	–
Total (professions	27	44	2	4	41	2	26	34	2
Small business	–	–	–	–	–	–	2	1	–
Director	14	2	1	4	2	–	30	1	1
Banker/financier	1	–	–	1	–	–	2	–	–
Executive/management	2	8	–	1	4	–	6	2	–
Commercie/insurance	3	1	–	–	–	–	6	–	–
Business consultant	1	2	1	–	1	1	4	1	–
Clerical	–	2	–	–	–	–	1	2	–
Total (business)	21	15	2	6	7	1	51	7	1
White collar	1	3	–	–	6	–	–	6	–
Political worker	1	2	–	–	–	–	–	1	–
Trade union official	–	9	–	–	2	–	–	7	–
Farmer/landowner	11	1	2	–	–	1	3	–	–
Housewife	–	–	–	–	1	–	1	1	–
Student	–	–	–	–	–	–	–	–	1
Journalist/author	2	10	–	2	3	1	6	2	–
Public relations	1	2	–	1	2	–	4	2	–
Actor	–	–	–	–	1	–	–	–	–
Pilot	–	–	–	–	–	–	1	–	–
Policeman	–	–	–	–	–	–	–	–	–
Total (miscellaneous)	16	27	2	3	15	2	15	19	1
Railwayman	–	4	–	–	–	–	–	–	–
Miner	–	4	–	–	3	–	–	2	–
Skilled worker	–	8	–	–	3	–	–	2	–
Semi/unskilled worker	–	4	–	–	3	–	–	–	–
Total (workers)	0	20	0	0	9	0	0	4	0
INA	0	0	0	0	0	0	0	0	0
Grand Total	64	106	6	13	72	5	92	64	4

(Table continued overleaf)

69

Table 5.3 (continued)

| | Feb. 1974 | | | Oct. 1974 | | |
	Con	Lab	Oth	Con	Lab	Oth
Barrister	12	1	–	2	1	–
Solicitor	1	–	3	–	–	–
Ch.surveyor/engineer	–	–	–	–	–	1
Civil service/local govt.	1	1	–	–	2	–
Services	–	–	–	1	–	–
Diplomatic services	2	–	–	–	–	–
Lecturer	–	10	2	–	9	–
School teacher	1	6	2	–	2	3
Doctor/dentist	–	–	–	–	–	–
Ch.accountant/secretary	6	1	2	–	–	–
Scientific worker	–	1	–	–	–	–
Minister of religion	–	–	1	–	–	–
Social worker	–	–	–	–	2	–
Total (professions)	23	20	10	3	16	4
Small business	–	2	2	–	–	–
Director	14	1	1	3	–	2
Banker/financier	7	–	–	1	–	–
Executive/management	5	2	–	1	–	–
Commerce/insurance	–	–	–	–	–	–
Business consultant	4	1	1	–	–	–
Clerical	–	1	–	–	–	–
Total (business)	30	7	4	5	0	2
White collar	–	1	–	–	1	–
Political worker	3	2	–	–	2	–
Trade union official	–	3	–	–	1	–
Farmer/landowner	2	–	5	–	–	1
Housewife	–	–	–	–	–	–
Student	–	–	–	–	–	–
Journalist/author	4	2	2	–	1	–
Public relations	–	2	–	–	–	–
Actor	–	–	–	–	–	–
Pilot	–	–	–	–	–	–
Policeman	–	–	–	–	–	–
Total (miscellaneous)	9	10	7	0	5	1
Railwayman	–	–	–	–	–	–
Miner	–	1	–	–	–	–
Skilled worker	–	6	–	–	1	–
Semi/unskilled worker	–	2	–	–	–	–
Total (workers)	0	9	0	0	1	0
INA	0	0	0	0	0	0
Grand total	62	46	21	8	22	7

One final professional group worthy of mention is the teaching profession (including all levels of education from school to university). As a profession nationally, of course, they increase with the corresponding expansion of post-war education and some increase in their parliamentary number is to be expected as a matter of routine choice. No doubt the national increase does in fact explain their increase on the Conservative side of the House, from 6 in 1945 to 11 in October 1974. Plainly this meagre number is a stark contrast to the central position which this profession has come to occupy in the Parliamentary Labour Party.

In turning to the business group we discover the cornerstone of the Conservative Party at Westminster. Not only does the business group provide the largest number of Conservatives but the overwhelming majority of this group falls within the category of company directors. In itself, this description means little since a company encompasses a wide size range from small businesses to vast enterprises. However, the extent of Conservatives' involvement with commerce and capital is not a primary concern here. For those fascinated with this question there are much more detailed and frequently entertaining sources [11]. The definition 'company director' has been applied only to those who were principally remunerated for such employment prior to their election: it does not record those who subsequently assumed directorships when at Westminster, when it is far from rare for politicians of all parties to become active in the business world [12].

During these thirty years 273 company directors were elected to Parliament; of these 245 were Conservatives. It is by far the largest single occupation represented at Westminster. They include Members with limited business connections and those with networks of business enterprises. They spread over the whole range of economic life and perhaps just one area is worthy of particular comment. The Tory–Brewers alliance which was forged by Gladstonian licensing legislation in the early 1870s has endured. It proved possible to trace 25 Conservatives in this period who had direct connections with brewing interests. One further Conservative had complementary interests in that he was a director of a leading potato crisp manufacturer. It is reassuring that the interests of sobriety were not neglected and another Conservative was a director of a tea company, and the House was even blessed with a Labour Temperance worker in the years immediately following the War.

There are some instructive conclusions to be drawn from the size of the business group in successive cohorts (Figure 5.2). Although there is some contraction in the middle cohorts, (the minimum being 36·5 per cent in 1964 due to a 32·8 per cent new intake of businessmen) the last four elections have revived the fortunes of business recruits in the Conservative Party and the last figure, in October 1974, represents the largest proportion at these ten elections. Especially notable are the new recruits. The two elections of 1974 returned business groups reaching 48·4 per cent and 62·5 per cent respectively (Figure 5.2). Obviously new recruits at these elections would be returned in better Conservative seats which suggests a distinctly improved position for the business group. Throughout the thirty years, they have been the most important source of Conservative politicians, but not only has this position been held, it has been advanced both in terms of backbench recruitment

(a) All Conservatives

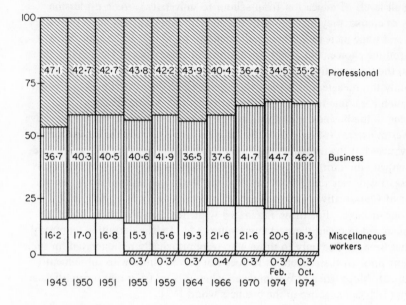

(b) New Conservatives

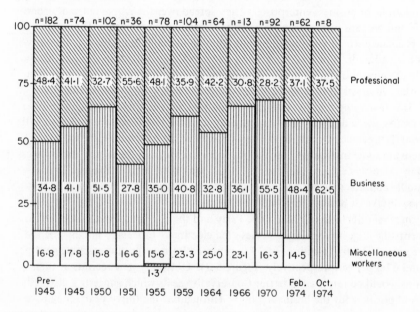

Figure 5.2   Occupational groupings of Conservatives, by cohort (percentages)

and leadership positions [13].

Before leaving the business section, a glance might be directed towards the fortunes of the small businessmen. Small businesses in the UK produce some 20 per cent of our industrial output, but they plainly are less successful in their output of political manpower. The ten elections brought the return of a mere eleven small businessmen, and of these the majority, seven, sat on the Labour side of the House.

The miscellaneous section is by definition a collection of occupations which do not easily fit elsewhere, and within this group the two important Conservative backgrounds are farming and journalism. Over the period as a whole, some 82 farmers and 34 journalists were elected to the Conservative benches. Farming, or more frequently landownership, represents the third most prolific source of Conservative MPs. Slightly over 10 per cent of Conservatives were primarily engaged in farming prior to election. However, the fate of this group has been considerably worse than the business group and, indeed, the success of the former largely explains the demise of the latter. Businessmen are to a degree displacing the farmers and landowners. (Tables 5.3 and 9.5 and Figure 5.3). In 1966,

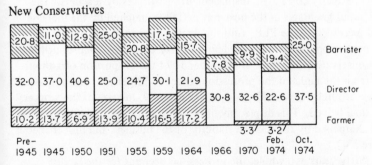

Figure 5.3   Some major Conservative occupations (percentages)

13·6 per cent of the party were farmers, but by October 1974 this figure was reduced to 8·1 per cent. This change is even clearer in the same four cohorts of new Conservatives. Since 1966 only five new Conservative farmers have been elected to the Commons (Table 5.3). The journalist group in this party – which ranges from newspaper journalists through television broadcasters and producers to authors – has been reasonably stable.

Overall, then, the Conservative Party in Parliament has not changed substantially in terms of the occupational backgrounds from which its Members have been recruited. The established professions of law, medicine, accountancy and the services consistently provide a considerable proportion of the party personnel. However, since 1966 the numbers of this group has decreased somewhat. A large part of the explanation for this is to be found in the failure to replace those MPs with an armed, or diplomatic, service background who departed over the last decade (Tables 5.3 and 9.5). Farming also has a traditional importance in the ranks of the parliamentary party, especially in the rural constituencies, but it has been apparently less favoured in the last ten years also. In contrast to farming and the professions, business (directors, executives and financiers) have fared well over the last four elections. The business ethic which symbolised the Conservative leadership during Mr Heath's Government, 1970–74, is reflected over the same period in recruitment to the Conservative benches. And whilst this change in Conservative recruitment has occurred on a much lesser scale than the transformation of the socio-economic composition of the Parliamentary Labour Party, it would be an omission to overlook this subtle re-drawing of the Conservative Party's occupational portrait.

Labour: from men of toil to men of ideas

The most distinctive feature about Labour MPs' pre-parliamentary occupational backgrounds over these three decades is the evidence which they furnish about the process and rate of embourgeoisement. In the simplest of terms there is a progressive, and almost perfectly correlated, displacement of workers by teachers. The expansion of Labour graduates in the post-war period is matched by the increase of professional recruits into the PLP. And the degree of change is such that the proportion of professional recruits in the Labour Party overtakes the proportion of equivalent Conservatives in 1966. By October 1974 the proportion of Labour MPs recruited from the ranks of the professions exceeds 50 per cent and surpasses the Conservative group by a clear 15 per cent. Conversely, the size of the workers' group is more than halved. This displacement of the workers group by the professional group is sharpened by the relative stability of the business and miscellaneous sections (Figure 5.4).

Taking the thirty years as a whole, the professions account for the largest segment of the Labour Party at Westminster (Figure 5.1). The overall proportions in the four groupings are: professions 40·7 per cent; business 9·6 per cent; miscellaneous 28·6 per cent; workers 21·1 per cent. Immediately this suggests a greater heterogeneity than the Conservative Party, where over 80 per cent are drawn from business and the professions. In fact, this wider spread of recruitment is not limited

74

(a) All Labour

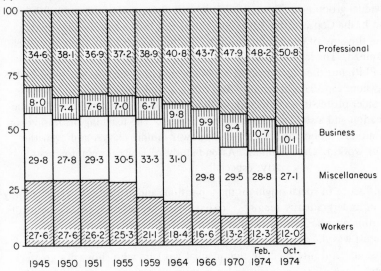

(b) New Labour

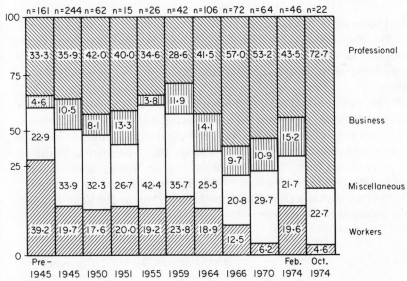

Figure 5.4   Occupational groupings of Labour, by cohort (percentages)

to more balanced groupings but also occurs in the range of particular occupations within individual groupings. This is especially well illustrated in the case of the professions. In the Conservative Party law, the armed forces and the diplomatic services form the core of professional recruits; in the Labour Party there is a much more even spread. The legal profession is again well represented (a steady 12 per cent of the PLP), but the older professions of law and medicine are balanced by the newer professions especially teaching. And this is a vital distinction, since admission to the older professions is much more likely to follow from traditional public school education and a solid middle class background. The teaching professions on the other hand are a popular choice for the lower middle classes and even the rising sons of working class families. As one study of graduate employment intimates:

> The influence of social origin on the aspirations and attitudes towards employment of undergraduates seems . . . to have been just as strong at the point of graduation as it had earlier been at the outset of undergraduate studies . . . The result was the underrepresentation in education of the graduate sons of professional and intermediate non-manual workers who showed a greater tendency than other graduates to be in private practice and commerce. On the other hand men with manual working fathers were particularly likely to be in education and were only rarely to be found in, for example, the legal profession, general management or the administrative class of the Home Civil Service. These emerged as notably socially exclusive sectors of graduate employment. [14]

In the Labour Party, therefore, the professions encompass two different social milieu — the established upper middle class and those who have transferred from one class to the next higher social class. The dramatic increase in the number of Labour professionals is almost wholly attributable to the rise of these Labour meritocrats.

At the first election listed here, 34·6 per cent of Labour MPs were drawn from the ranks of the professions (Figure 5.4): they included 46 barristers and solicitors and 47 teachers and lecturers. By October 1974 the strength of the professions in the PLP measured some 50·8 per cent of the party. But if the group is divided into separate occupations (Table 5.2), we find at this later election 38 barristers and solicitors and 89 teachers and lecturers. Adjusting the figures to take account of the different parliamentary strengths of the Labour Party in 1945 and October 1974, the following results emerge:

	1945	Oct. 1974	Difference
Professional group	34·6	50·8	+16·2
Barristers/solicitors	11·9	12·0	+ 0·1
Teachers/lecturers	12·1	28·1	+16·5

Thus the increased professional group on the Labour benches is explained by the growth of one particular profession – the teachers and lecturers – who have extended their parliamentary representation by 136 per cent over these ten elections. The other Labour professional occupations have remained reasonably stable.

The business group is the least numerically important of Labour occupations. During these thirty years businessmen comprise between 6·7 per cent and 10·7 per cent of the parliamentary party, and there is some evidence to suggest that they are less likely to be adopted in Labour's better seats. In sharp contrast to Conservatives, Labour's business group is spread throughout the various commercial occupations and not largely limited to company directors and financiers. Middle-management is the largest single category, followed by company directors, clerical staff and business consultants. Thus, besides being much less numerous than in the Conservative Party, Labour's recruits from the commercial and business world are employed (at least prior to their election) in less prominent positions.

In the Labour Party, the miscellaneous group largely comprises three occupations – journalists, white collar workers and trade union officials. The journalists are frequently, like the teachers, examples of Labour meritocrats and tend to have lower middle class or working class origins (as indicated by their educational backgrounds). But the key occupation here is trade union official, and 98 union officials were returned at these ten elections. This represents 11·6 per cent of all Labour Members [15]. For the most part these MPs achieve entry later in life and are less likely to achieve government office. Moreover they have been, in contrast to actual manual workers, a relatively stable group within the PLP, although since 1959 this group has suffered some reduction (Figure 5.5). (Since union officials most frequently appear in better seats, which tends to delay the effect of displacement, this reduction can be most easily seen by reference to the last five cohorts of new Labour MPs.)

However, there can be no mistaking the predominant trend in the case of manual workers. As a whole, they account for over one-fifth of Labour MPs, but at each election since 1945 they have suffered consistent and considerable depletion. In 1945 they comprised 27·6 per cent of Labour's parliamentarians, but by the last election in this period they had been reduced to a mere 12 per cent. If we compare these figures with the rising fortunes of the teaching profession – increasing from 12·1 per cent to 28·1 per cent – it is plain just how remarkably closely the fortunes of the teaching and working occupations are correlated. The step by step increase of teachers almost perfectly matches the step by step decrease of manual workers. In the first half of this period not only do workers form the backbone of the PLP, they are clearly allocated Labour's better seats (see especially the 1959 new cohort). From the beginning of this period, middle class candidates captured many of Labour's non-sponsored seats, but from 1964 even Labour's strongholds have been wrested from the workers by Labour's new professional men. It has caused one Welsh miner MP to make the observation: 'In our party you now need callouses on your backside instead of your hands' [16]. Indeed by 1971 Labour's national

All Labour

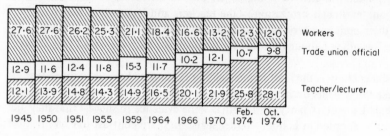

Workers
Trade union official

Teacher/lecturer

1945 1950 1951 1955 1959 1964 1966 1970 Feb.1974 Oct.1974

New Labour

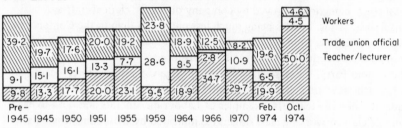

Workers
Trade union official
Teacher/lecturer

Pre–1945 1945 1950 1951 1955 1959 1964 1966 1970 Feb.1974 Oct.1974

Figure 5.5   Some major Labour occupations

agent was making the remarkable complaint that 'we could do with many more MPs of the artisan/craftsman type' [17]. Of all constituencies the mining ones have been least attracted to this new breed of Labour candidates; but the future representation of even some of these will be tested at the next election when a number of Labour's miners are expected to retire. The chairman of the miners' MPs, Dennis Skinner, has no doubts in his mind about the propriety of non-miners in the traditional mining constituencies:

> Whereas, in previous years (before, say, 1955) constituencies with strong mining connections generally accepted the idea of a mining candidate without too much demur, in the last two decades the scramble to obtain a parliamentary seat by travelling Westminster-mongers has, to say the least, become a little undignified. The result is a plethora of smooth-tongued, generally tall, dark, handsome men (not women) percolating and permeating their way around the slag heaps, up and down the terraced rows of colliery houses and into the miners' welfare to see the branch officials, sometimes assisted by over-zealous Party organisers — many of these splendid, would-be parliamentarians weave a series of ten minute speeches out of a concoction of the 1926 strike; the beauty of pigeon and whippet racing; *How Green was my Valley* and grandfather's long cherished pit helmet and safety lamp! [18]

Quite clearly, fellow-feeling is taken to be no substitute for actual mining experience.

The fact that many of Labour's new men from the professions can claim working class origins and their position be explained by upward social mobility [19] does not really change the fact that the workers themselves, who historically and ideologically have played such a fundamental role in the Labour Party, are rapidly being removed from Labour's parliamentary ranks. The rate of displacement is modified by the workers presently at Westminster holding safe constituencies, but the next couple of elections are likely to witness further blows to the manual workers. Although they are unlikely to disappear altogether, few new workers are arriving at Westminster. At the last four elections only 23 of the 204 new Labour MPs were workers. On current trends it seems reasonable to expect the manual workers in the PLP to have fallen to between 5 and 10 per cent in another decade and a half — and these few will owe their success to the intransigence of the mining and a few other unions, in retaining a distinct preference for representatives of their own kind.

Minor parties

As with their educational groupings, the collection of minor party MPs display a wide range of occupational backgrounds. The Liberal Party has some connections with the world of business, several of its number claiming company directorships. Barristers, accountants, journalists, teachers and a doctor are among others also included in this group. It tends, in practice, to be a mix of established professions and business and not greatly dissimilar to the Conservative profile. The United Ulster Unionists are a wider social mix. They include established and new professions, and where business is represented it is invariably at a lower level than in the Conservative Party and more closely resembles Liberal business connections. This party is the one party where small businessmen appear, *pro rata*, in any significant number. The Nationalist Parties are a mix of teachers, lawyers, businessmen, farmers and journalists. The newer professions are much in evidence and there is a particularly high proportion of school teachers.

Conclusion

Overall, the dramatic decline of worker representatives has been the singular most striking feature of parliamentary recruitment during these thirty years. Indeed, if paid trade union officials are separated from practising manual workers this decline is even greater than other studies have recognised. The Nuffield Election series, for example, lumps these two groups together and suggests a decline from 38 per cent to 28 per cent — a reduction of between one-third and one-quarter. However, the actual workers decline from 27·6 per cent in 1945 to 12 per cent in October 1974 — a reduction of more than half. Moreover, this trend shows every sign of continuing and even accelerating.

It is again tempting to contemplate the convergence thesis which postulates movement towards a common recruiting ground for all political parties somewhere in the region of the middle and upper-middle classes. There is some substance to this argument since quite clearly the workers in the Labour Party are being replaced by middle class professional recruits. However, in the same way that the strong association between the Conservative Party and the public schools remains a crucial difference in the educational profiles of the two major parliamentary parties, there remain vital differences in the socio-economic composition of the parties at Westminster as expressed in their occupational profiles. Changes within the two major parties themselves should not be allowed to blur important disparities. The Conservative Party at Westminster is a much more socially and economically harmonious group. There has been a noticeable drift from the land to commerce, but it is still a party with a largely common background. Even the distinction between the professions and business is much modified by the involvement of many of the former group in commercial undertakings, if not before election, certainly subsequent to entering the Commons. The Labour Party, in contrast, has three distinct centres of occupational background – the established professions, the newer professions and the workers. The former group, who most closely resemble the Conservatives and tend to be the liberals in the party, are drawn from solid middle class backgrounds. At the other extreme are the manual group of pure working class abstraction who as a group, have occupied a central role in the development of the Labour Party. In between these two, and displacing the latter, are the newer professions and although many of these are first generation middle class, owing their new status to recent social elevation, they are clearly not actual representatives of the working classes but neither are they identical to the established professions, as sociologists and the Registrar Generals' occupational groupings recognise. Without doubt, the Parliamentary Labour Party has undergone a vital social transformation in recent years, but this in itself is not sufficient to equate with converging recruitment patterns. The Conservative Party remains homogeneous; the Labour Party remains heterogeneous. What is happening in the PLP is that the men of toil are being rapidly replaced by the men of ideas.

Notes

[1] I. Jennings, *Parliament*, 2nd ed., Oxford University Press, London, 1957, p. 58.

[2] Ross, op cit., p. 434.

[3] David V. Fleischer, *Thirty Years of Legislative Recruitment in Brazil*, paper delivered at the 10th World Congress of the International Political Science Association, Edinburgh, 1976. I am indebted to Professor Fleischer, of the Universidade de Brasilia, for permission to quote from this paper.

[4] A full explanation is given in Chapter 1.

[5] See in particular the Nuffield figures.

[6] Julian Critchley, *New Statesman*, 5th February 1965. See also, R.W. Johnson, op. cit., (1973), pp. 45–8; 56–9; p. 74. and N.W. Ellis, *Dear Elector*, Coronet, London, 1974, pp. 24–6.

[7] J. Blondel, *Voters, Parties, Leaders*, Penguin, London, 1974, p. 142.

[8] Compared with Labour barristers, twice as many Conservative barristers achieve appointment as Queen's Counsel.

[9] Rush, op. cit., p. 73.

[10] It should, of course, be noted that this decline corresponds with a decline in regular service personnel. It is easy to confuse cause and effect.

[11] Outstanding here are the successive publications by Andrew Roth: *The Business Background of MPs* and (with J. Kerby) *The MPs' Chart and the MPs' Gallery*, Parliamentary Profiles, London. These precede the much less enjoyable reading of the recent Register of MPs' Interests. See also on this question, R.W. Johnson, op. cit., pp. 56–9.

[12] Roth refers to a theory of 'inheritance of acquired directorships' or 'political Lysenkoism', *Business Background of MPs*, 1966, p. xii.

[13] Johnson, op. cit., p. 52. The businessmen who were prominent in Heath's Conservative Cabinet 1970–74 have been replaced on Mrs Thatcher's Front Bench by men of different ethics but not so radically different abstraction.

[14] R.K. Kelsall et al., *Times Higher Education Supplement*, 25th February 1972.

[15] These are the MPs who were principally employed as trade union officials and many others held some position in a trade union but were principally engaged in other occupations. See Chapter 7.

[16] Quoted in Roth, op. cit., p. xix.

[17] *Sunday Times*, 3rd January 1971.

[18] Dennis Skinner MP, 'We need more of our own kind in Parliament', *The Miner*, September–October, 1976. I am indebted to Mr Skinner for permission to quote from this article.

[19] There has also been a slight shrinkage of the proportion of the British people employed in manual trades.

6 Amateurs and professionals

Career politicians

For some, the occasion of their first election to Parliament will mark the beginning of a protracted parliamentary career. These are the career politicians who will generally remain MPs until their retirement. They comprise the group from whom government offices are usually filled and a number of them may well find their active political career further extended, beyond retirement from the Commons, by later elevation to the House of Lords. For others, however, election will simply allow a brief taste of parliamentary life. Electoral success will be limited to one or, at most, two victories and higher political aspirations will be impeded by the shortness of their stay at Westminster. Government office will be almost invariably denied them. For these MPs, Parliament is an interval, not a career. Thus, there are two types of MPs — those who win an isolated election and those who become career politicians. The terms *amateurs* and *professionals* have been used to distinguish these two breeds of politicians [1].

The criterion for distinguishing professionals from amateurs can take the form of either counting electoral victories or measuring the duration of parliamentary service: both have been used. Philip Buck, in his study of British MPs between 1918 and 1959 chose the former approach and proposed that: ' . . . on the occasion of his third election a contestant loses amateur standing and becomes a professional' [2]. Donald Matthews also identified different political career patterns in his study of American senators, but favoured the 'length of service' approach, the demarcation between amateur and professional being ten or more years in public office [3]. In practice, the two approaches do not produce dissimilar results as both approaches employ the notion of professionalism to signify a commitment to a reasonably lasting legislative career on the part of the politician, combined, of course, with the electoral security that is necessary to fulfil that commitment.

Of these two approaches, the one favouring tenure of office is used in this study, and professionals are defined as those MPs who have served ten or more years at Westminster. Given the intervals between elections, this will mean that, except in a few rare cases of interrupted careers, they will all have won at least three elections. Those who fall by the wayside remain amateurs. If anything, this might be a slightly more stringent approach, given the proximity of some post-war elections. Buck's criterion, for example, would describe as professional those MPs who won their third consecutive election in October 1974, even though they had first entered the Commons only just over four years earlier. But if the word professional conveys the connotation of being well-experienced in the practice of parliamentary politics, perhaps the duration of service is more indicative of this skill than electoral successes.

Approximately two-thirds of MPs do become professionals, and spend a decade or more in the House of Commons. This proportion is the same in both the Conservative and Labour Parties. Not surprisingly, minor parties, since they do not hold such safe constituencies, have had fewer career politicians and more amateurs. By the time of the October 1974 General Election exactly the same number of Conservative and Labour MPs had attained 'professional' status — 436 in both parties. Of the 83 minor party MPs, just 27 had gained this distinction [4]. At the other end of the scale, one-third serve for less than ten years, the majority of these winning only one general election. Obviously the most important factor in determining who will become a career politician is the allocation of safe seats. Adoption in a safe seat, provided that the candidate is not nominated too late in life and that he retains the confidence of his constituency party, will ensure that he attains professional status in the due course of events.

Table 6.1
Parliamentary service of all MPs, by cohort

	1945		1950		1951		1955		1959	
Years	MPs	%	MPs	%	MPs	%	MPs	%	MPs	%
0–4	397	61·9	173	27·7	202	32·2	154	24·4	216	34·2
5–9	65	10·2	277	44·3	251	40·2	162	25·8	166	26·4
10–19	140	21·9	122	19·5	112	18·0	237	37·6	192	30·5
20–29	35	5·5	46	7·4	56	9·0	65	10·3	47	7·5
30+	3	0·5	7	1·1	4	0·6	12	1·9	9	1·4
Total	640	100·0	625	100·0	625	100·0	630	100·0	630	100·0

	1964		1966		1970		Feb. 1974		Oct. 1974	
Years	MPs	%	MPs	%	MPs	%	MPs	%	MPs	%
0–4	182	28·9	245	38·9	210	33·3	251	39·5	278	43·8
5–9	162	25·7	111	17·6	152	24·2	75	11·8	75	11·8
10–19	239	37·9	171	27·1	160	25·4	219	34·5	201	31·7
20–29	38	6·1	93	14·8	101	16·0	88	13·9	79	12·4
30+	9	1·4	10	1·6	7	1·1	2	0·3	2	0·3
Total	630	100·0	630	100·0	630	100·0	635	100·0	635	100·0

The actual patterns of parliamentary service during this period will naturally be coloured by the unique phenomenon of 1945 when there was such a massive influx of newly elected MPs. They created an almost tidal progression which sweeps through Parliament during these thirty years (Table 6.1). At the 1955, 1959 and 1964 elections, these MPs had attained professional status and had served between ten and nineteen years. By the 1966 election, they had completed twenty-one years service, and by the 1974 elections, those post-war veterans who remained were on the verge of completing their thirtieth year in Parliament, with ten successive election victories behind them. Naturally, however, by the mid-sixties many of them were reaching retirement age. Although politics is one of the few professions which has no mandatory retirement age, constituency parties and, where sponsorship is involved, trade unions often have definite ideas about when their MPs should retire. Consequently, quite a number of them did retire in 1966 and 1970, and a fresh influx of new Members appeared to replace them.

Table 6.2
Parlimentary service of Conservative MPs

(a) All Conservatives

Years	1945		1950		1951		1955		1959	
	MPs	%	MPs	%	MPs	%	MPs	%	MPs	%
0–4	98	45·9	105	35·4	136	42·4	110	32·1	158	43·0
5–9	34	16·0	84	28·3	73	22·8	94	27·4	112	30·7
10–19	62	29·1	80	27·0	71	22·3	96	28·0	63	17·5
20–29	16	7·5	21	7·1	36	11·3	36	10·5	27	7·4
30+	3	1·5	7	2·2	4	1·2	7	2·0	5	1·4
Total	213	100·0	297	100·0	320	100·0	343	100·0	365	100·0

Years	1964		1966		1970		Feb. 1974		Oct. 1974	
	MPs	%	MPs	%	MPs	%	MPs	%	MPs	%
0–4	65	21·6	59	23·3	107	32·4	121	40·8	120	43·3
5–9	105	34·9	71	28·1	76	23·0	25	8·4	24	8·7
10–19	105	34·9	93	36·7	100	30·4	110	37·0	98	35·4
20–29	23	7·6	27	10·7	43	13·0	41	13·8	35	12·6
30+	3	1·0	3	1·2	4	1·2	–	–	–	–
Total	301	100·0	253	100·0	330	100·0	297	100·0	277	100·0

(b) Departing Conservatives

Years	1945		1950		1951		1955		1959	
	MPs	%	MPs	%	MPs	%	MPs	%	MPs	%
0–4	16	35·6	4	16·7	10	17·9	15	18·1	38	33·0
5–9	9	20·0	10	41·7	12	21·3	20	24·1	36	31·3
10–19	15	33·3	6	25·0	22	39·3	22	26·5	23	20·0
20–29	5	11·1	2	8·3	10	17·9	21	25·3	15	13·1
30+	–	–	2	8·3	2	3·6	5	6·0	3	2·6
Total	45	100·0	24	100·0	56	100·0	83	100·0	115	100·0

Years	1964		1966		1970		Feb. 1974	
	MPs	%	MPs	%	MPs	%	MPs	%
0–4	3	5·6	2	4·8	20	22·7	10	30·3
5–9	16	29·6	10	23·8	3	3·4	3	9·1
10–19	21	38·9	19	45·3	34	38·6	13	39·4
20–29	12	22·2	11	26·1	24	27·3	7	21·2
30+	2	3·7	–	–	7	8·0	–	–
Total	54	100·0	42	100·0	88	100·0	33	100·0

Table 6.3
Parliamentary service of Labour MPs

(a) All Labour

Years	1945 MPs	%	1950 MPs	%	1951 MPs	%	1955 MPs	%	1959 MPs	%
0–4	289	72·2	63	20·0	61	20·7	41	14·8	57	22·1
5–9	26	6·5	189	60·0	176	59·7	65	23·5	51	19·8
10–19	67	16·8	41	13·0	39	13·2	138	49·8	127	49·3
20–29	18	4·5	22	7·0	19	6·4	28	10·1	20	7·7
30+	–	–	–	–	–	–	5	1·8	3	1·1
Total	400	100·0	315	100·0	295	100·0	277	100·0	258	100·0

Years	1964 MPs	%	1966 MPs	%	1970 MPs	%	Feb. 1974 MPs	%	Oct. 1974 MPs	%
0–4	111	34·7	176	48·1	97	33·5	102	33·9	128	40·2
5–9	56	17·5	39	10·7	74	25·5	46	15·3	47	14·7
10–19	132	41·2	77	21·1	59	20·3	106	35·1	100	31·3
20–29	15	4·7	66	18·2	57	19·7	45	15·0	42	13·2
30+	6	1·9	7	1·9	3	1·0	2	0·7	2	0·6
Total	320	100·0	365	100·0	290	100·0	301	100·0	319	100·0

(b) Departing Labour

Years	1945 MPs	%	1950 MPs	%	1951 MPs	%	1955 MPs	%	1959 MPs	%
0–4	84	63·6	5	13·5	4	8·2	3	4·8	6	10·8
5–9	9	6·8	23	62·2	32	65·3	9	14·5	5	8·9
10–19	30	22·8	6	16·2	7	14·3	34	54·8	36	64·1
20–29	9	6·8	3	8·1	6	12·2	11	17·8	6	10·8
30+	–	–	–	–	–	–	5	8·1	3	5·4
Total	132	100·0	37	100·0	49	100·0	62	100·0	56	100·0

Years	1964 MPs	%	1966 MPs	%	1970 MPs	%	Feb. 1974 MPs	%
0–4	2	8·0	50	42·7	5	10·2	1	9·1
5–9	3	12·0	–	–	4	8·2	1	9·1
10–19	15	60·0	28	23·9	13	26·5	5	45·5
20–29	3	12·0	33	28·2	25	51·0	4	36·3
30+	2	8·0	6	5·2	2	4·1	–	–
Total	25	100·0	117	100·0	49	100·0	11	100·0

The patterns of parliamentary service in the two major parties also reflect the impact of the 1945 intake, and differ little (Tables 6.2 and 6.3). Not including 1945, in both parties the size of the 0–4 years group is at its lowest when a party loses a general election and thus finds less of its displaced Members (either through defeat or retirement) being replaced. At the other end of the scale, the gradual growth in the number of professionals in the 1950s and 1960s is fairly clear. Indeed, this is probably most easily illustrated by the significantly large proportion of Labour MPs in 1966 and 1970 with over twenty years service to their credit. By 1974, retirements began to reduce the number of these longstanding MPs, although they still form an important core of the PLP. It is to be expected that an even larger number will not seek re-election next time, which will in turn further deplete the remainder of these veteran parliamentarians. The number of MPs in both parties who have served for over thirty years are a mere handful. Any survivors of 1945 who do, in fact, seek re-election next time will join this distinguished group.

The data on the service of departing MPs is fairly self-evident. However, it is worth recalling that 'departing' is used here to describe an MP winning his last general election. Hence, for example, a departing MP listed in the 1966 cohort, won his last general election in that year, but may not have actually left Parliament until 1970.

Table 6.4
Parliamentary service of minor party MPs

(a) All MPs

Years	1945	1950	1951	1955	1959	1964	1966	1970	Feb. 1974	Oct. 1974
0–4	10	5	5	3	1	6	10	6	28	30
5–9	5	4	2	3	3	1	1	2	4	4
10–19	11	1	2	3	2	2	1	1	3	3
20–29	1	3	1	1	–	–	–	1	2	2
30+	–	–	–	–	1	–	–	–	–	–
Total	27	13	10	10	7	9	12	10	37	39

(b) Departing MPs

Years	1945	1950	1951	1955	1959	1964	1966	1970 Feb. 1974	Feb 1974 Oct. 1974
0–4	8	2	1	2	–	1	4	1	2
5–9	4	1	–	1	2	–	–	1	1
10–19	8	–	1	1	1	1	–	–	2
20–29	1	1	–	–	–	–	–	–	–
30+	–	–	–	–	1	–	–	–	–
Total	21	4	2	4	4	2	4	2	5

As would be expected, there have been fewer professional parliamentarians in the minor parties (Table 6.4). Quite simply they have been denied the electoral security to survive in Parliament for long periods. Many of those who served for more than ten years, did so at the beginning of this period. It remains to be seen whether the Nationalists who entered in 1974 will still be at Westminster in ten years time, or whether they will have switched their attentions towards newly created Scottish and Welsh Assemblies. The only MP from the minor parties who remained in the Commons for more than thirty years was Clement Davies, Liberal MP for Montgomery and, until his death, leader of the Liberal Party.

In the ten elections between 1918 and 1951, it has been calculated that the average length of parliamentary service was 6·3 years. [5] Since 1945, it is clear that this average has increased (Table 6.5). In 1945, the figure was 5·3 years, by 1966 it was 10·1 years, and the figure has not fallen below nine years since 1955. In the whole of the interwar years, the highest average was 8·1 years, in 1935. The last six elections have plainly returned on average, a more experienced group of parliamentarians than at any election since 1918. The 1966 Parliament, in particular, appears to have been especially rich in mature parliamentarians, and again this is largely explained by the presence of a core of MPs remaining from 1945. However, the number of these who have retired in recent years is illustrated by the increasing average service of departing MPs at the last four elections. Their influence is especially noticeable in the 1970 cohort (i.e., those MPs who left at, or shortly before, the February 1974 General Election).

Table 6.5
Average parliamentary service

(a) All MPs

		1945	1950	1951	1955	1959	1964	1966	1970	Feb. 1974	Oct. 1974
Con	No. MPs	213	297	320	343	365	301	253	330	297	277
	Total service	1538	2402	2529	2939	3027	2944	2801	3060	3029	2576
	Average	7·2	8·1	7·9	8·6	8·3	9·8	11·1	9·3	10·2	9·3
Lab	No. MPs	400	315	295	277	258	320	365	290	301	319
	Total service	1623	2234	2226	2789	2913	3175	3549	2777	3162	2995
	Average	4·1	7·1	7·5	10·1	11·3	9·9	9·6	9·5	10·5	9·4
Oth	No. MPs	27	13	10	10	7	9	12	10	37	39
	Total service	221	101	62	84	84	42	37	53	151	140
	Average	8·2	7·8	6·2	8·4	12·0	4·9	3·1	5·3	4·1	3·6
All	No. MPs	640	625	630	630	630	630	630	630	635	635
	Total service	3402	4737	4817	5812	6024	6161	6387	/5890	6342	5711
	Average	5·3	7·6	7·7	9·2	9·6	9·7	10·1	9·4	10·0	9·0

(b) Departing MPs

		1945	1950	1951	1955	1959	1964	1966	1970	Feb. 1974
Con	No. MPs	45	24	56	83	115	54	42	88	33
	Total service	362	264	697	1094	1194	784	600	1428	403
	Average	8·0	11·0	12·4	13·2	10·4	14·5	14·3	16·2	12·2

(Table continued overleaf)

Table 6.5 (continued)

(b) Departing MPs

		1945	1950	1951	1955	1959	1964	1966	1970	Feb. 1974
Lab	No. MPs	132	37	49	62	56	25	138	49	11
	Total service	822	289	466	854	795	413	1432	947	176
	Average	6·2	7·8	9·5	13·8	14·2	16·5	10·3	19·3	16·0
Oth	No. MPs	21	4	2	4	4	2	6	2	5
	Total service	146	26	10	24	61	19	8	9	32
	Average	6·9	6·5	5·0	6·0	15·3	9·5	1·3	4·5	6·4

Conclusion

Clearly the distinction which Buck made between amateur and professional MPs has remained valid throughout this post-war period. The amateurs win only isolated elections and remain at Westminster for probably five or less years. They may be less committed to a life of politics than the career politicians or simply unable to win nomination in a secure constituency. One of the unfortunate effects of party politics is that an MP's tenure in the House of Commons is related not to his own skills and ability, but rather the performance of party leaderships. Come election time, the electorate judge his colleagues collectively, not him individually. Those who have achieved professional status, however, generally survive in Parliament for nearer twenty years, and quite a few remain for twenty-five or more years.

The professionals make two important contributions to parliamentary politics. Firstly, they comprise the vast majority of office holders. Buck calculated that in the period 1918–1959, 72·6 per cent of all government posts and 98·4 per cent of all Cabinet ministries were held by MPs who had achieved professional status. There are, of course, exceptions to this general principle, when a party might find a specific constituency for someone whom they wish to include in their Government [6]. Also, in the case of the Labour Party, the prospects of government office are not quite so closely linked as they are in the Conservative Party with factors such as ease of initial election and the extent of a Member's service.

Their second contribution is equally important, although somewhat less publicised. This is their work in the day-to-day business of the House of Commons. In appointing MPs to Select Committees, for example, the party whips tend to apply, unofficially at least, a seniority principle. It means that senior MPs frequently occupy key positions in the committee structure of the House, and while Commons' committees are much less powerful than their American Congressional equivalents, they retain considerable prestige and moral authority. Furthermore, the subtle influence of the parliamentary elders, both within the House and through the party machines, can sometimes be under-estimated in accounts of Westminster politics.

But undoubtedly the most significant feature in this analysis of parliamentary service is the impact created by the massive influx of 1945. These MPs have been at the centre of parliamentary life throughout this period, and especially so in the case of the Labour Party. The present Labour Prime Minister, James Callaghan, and his two predecessors as Labour leaders, Sir Harold Wilson and Hugh Gaitskell, all entered Parliament in the spectacular victory of 1945. Throughout, this group have been a central force in the shaping of Labour ideas and the appointment of leading figures in the PLP. The fact, therefore, that the size of the 1945 group begins to decline quite markedly by the late sixties and early seventies has important implications for the Labour Party. After the next election there will probably be but a handful of these Labour veterans remaining. The new Labour professionals will be the intakes of the 1960s. More importantly, they will by then have a near monopoly of leadership positions. The figures who have dominated the Labour Party for so many years will have been completely replaced by a new breed of Labour leaders.

Notes

[1] P.W. Buck, *Amateurs and Professionals in British Politics*, Chicago University Press, London, 1963. A similar classification is employed by Donald Matthews in *U.S. Senators and Their World*, Vintage Books, New York, 1960. In addition to *Amateurs and Professionals*, he describes those Senators from 'old families' as *Patricians* and those with little occupational attainment as *Agitators*.

[2] op. cit., p. 78.

[3] op. cit., pp. 58–61. In fact, Matthews is measuring political activity prior to Senate election, but the same approach can be transposed to fit activity in an elected legislative body.

[4] These figures are calculated by adding the number of departing MPs with ten or more years service to those with this qualification remaining in October 1974. Obviously, these figures will be increased in time by the addition of some who, although they had less than ten years to their credit in 1974, will in time become professionals.

[5] J.F.S. Ross, *Elections and Electors*, Eyre and Spottiswoode, London, 1955, p. 402.

[6] An example of this was when Wilson's Labour Government wished to include Frank Cousins, the Transport and General Workers' Union Leader, in the Cabinet, he was found a seat at Nuneaton in 1965. The only general election which he fought, and won, was in 1966. Similarly, John Davies, former leader of the Confederation of British Industry, an employers' association, won a place in Heath's Conservative Cabinet immediately after his first electoral victory at Knutsford in 1970.

7 Miscellaneous matters

Local government in Parliament [1]

One reason why Labour MPs have traditionally entered Parliament later in life than Conservatives is that many have found it necessary to serve a political apprenticeship before their party rewarded them with a safe parliamentary constituency to contest. This is especially true of working class representatives who have needed time to establish their status in the Labour movement. Frequently, this apprenticeship takes the form of local government service.

Membership of a local council is for most councillors the extent of their political ambitions. Studies of particular councils have generally shown that members rarely acquire parliamentary aspirations [2]. Nevertheless, since 1945 service on local authorities has become an increasingly important factor in parliamentary recruitment. A large proportion of Labour Members of Parliament, and an increasing proportion of Conservative MPs have used their membership of a local council as a stepping-stone towards Westminster. Of the 1,758 MPs elected at the ten general elections from 1945 to 1974, 617 – slightly over one-third of the total – had at some time before their first election been an elected member of a local authority (Table 7.1). This background has been particularly common among Labour Members of Parliament. Indeed, nearly half of the Labour Members elected since 1945 have held an elective office in municipal politics prior to their election to Parliament. Of the 860 Labour MPs, 470 are ex-councillors and approximately two-thirds of these had served on a county borough or borough authority. The Labour Party, as would be expected, is very much the party of urban government. In comparison, rather fewer Conservatives have taken the local council chamber route to Westminster: approximately a quarter of post-war Conservative MPs are ex-councillors.

The importance of community service in the recruitment of Labour MPs might be demonstrated in two further ways. There is evidence that not only are Labour Members of Parliament more likely than Conservatives to have been members of a local authority, but also that they have tended to have served a longer period on such a body before their initial election to Parliament. In the October 1974 Parliament, for example, the average length of council service of Labour MPs with this background was 9·3 years: the equivalent figure for Conservative Members was 6·9 years [3]. Similarly, the prevalence of community service in the early careers of Labour Members of Parliament is confirmed by the proportion of local magistrates among the Labour benches in the House of Commons during this period. Over 10 per cent of Labour MPs had previously been JPs, compared with 6 per cent of Conservatives. The significance of both these features – longer periods in municipal

Table 7.1

MPs with local government experience, 1945–1974

| Conservatives | | | Labour | | | Other | | | Total | | |
Council	MPs	%	Council	MPs	%	Council	MPs	%	Council	MPs	%
CB	50	6·1	CB	127	14·8	CB	3	3·6	CB	180	10·2
B	76	9·3	B	154	17·9	B	5	6·0	B	235	13·4
CC	66	8·1	CC	63	7·3	CC	6	7·3	CC	135	7·7
UDC	19	2·3	UDC	46	5·3	UDC	2	2·4	UDC	67	3·8
Total		25·8	Total		45·3	Total		19·3	Total		35·1
None	604	74·2	None	470	54·7	None	67	80·7	None	1141	64·9
Total	815	100·0	Total	860	100·0	Total	83	100·0	Total	1758	100·0

Note: UDC includes urban and rural district councils.

politics and service as a local magistrate – is that they are further evidence of the normal need in Labour circles to establish party status and political achievement before being elevated to a place in the more important representative positions.

The proportions of MPs in the major parties drawn from local government at successive elections are shown in Figure 7.1. In the case of the Labour Party, municipal backgrounds have been much in evidence throughout this period. At each general election, except 1959, more than 40 per cent of all Labour MPs have been recruited from the arena of local politics. And, despite the social transformation of the Parliamentary Labour Party which has taken place since 1945, this is one feature of Labour recruitment which has remained undisturbed. Indeed, the last two Parliaments have contained the two largest proportions of ex-councillors on the Labour benches. The predominance of local government in the selection of Labour parliamentary candidates is partly explained by the traditional nature and role of some constituency activists. W.J.M. Mackenzie noted many years ago that there is a 'close connection between the Labour Party representatives on the local authority and the party committees which choose parliamentary candidates' [4]. In the more solid Northern and Welsh Labour constituencies especially, this has manifested itself in the reward of nomination going to someone who has already displayed loyalty and service to the Party in municipal (or trade union) politics. This is the route taken by almost all the remaining Labour MPs with working class origins.

In the Conservative Party, there has been a distinct increase in the number who have followed the council chamber route to Westminster. In 1945, 14·1 per cent of all Conservative Members of Parliament had previously served as elected members of a local authority. By February 1974 this proportion had more than doubled to 32 per cent. The increase in the number of ex-borough representatives on this side of the House largely accounted for this trend. Throughout, a core of Conservative councillor MPs have been drawn from county councils, but during these thirty years the proportion of Conservative MPs who had served on a borough authority increased from 2·8 per cent to 15·5 per cent (Tables 7.2 and 7.3).

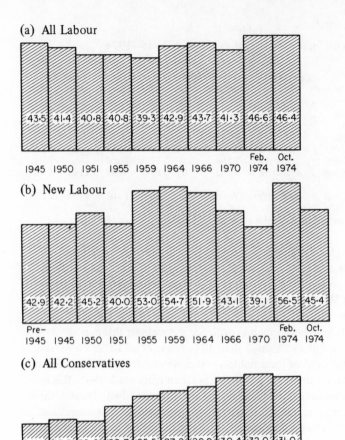

(a) All Labour

43.5 | 41.4 | 40.8 | 40.8 | 39.3 | 42.9 | 43.7 | 41.3 | 46.6 | 46.4

1945 1950 1951 1955 1959 1964 1966 1970 Feb. 1974 Oct. 1974

(b) New Labour

42.9 | 42.2 | 45.2 | 40.0 | 53.0 | 54.7 | 51.9 | 43.1 | 39.1 | 56.5 | 45.4

Pre-1945 1945 1950 1951 1955 1959 1964 1966 1970 Feb. 1974 Oct. 1974

(c) All Conservatives

14.1 | 16.8 | 16.6 | 20.7 | 25.5 | 27.2 | 28.9 | 30.4 | 32.0 | 31.0

1945 1950 1951 1955 1959 1964 1966 1970 Feb. 1974 Oct. 1974

(d) New Conservatives

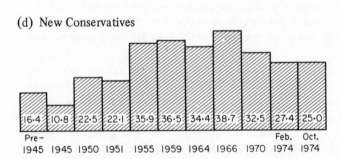

16.4 | 10.8 | 22.5 | 22.1 | 35.9 | 36.5 | 34.4 | 38.7 | 32.5 | 27.4 | 25.0

Pre-1945 1945 1950 1951 1955 1959 1964 1966 1970 Feb. 1974 Oct. 1974

Figure 7.1 Local government experience by cohort (percentages)

Table 7.2

Local government experience of all MPs, by election

		Conservative				Labour				Other	
Election	Total MPs	Coun-cil	No. MPs	%	Total MPs	Coun-cil	No. MPs	%	Total MPs	Coun-cil	No. MPs
1945	213	CB	9	4·2	400	CB	61	15·2	27	CB	1
		B	6	2·8		B	61	15·2		B	3
		CC	15	7·1		CC	37	9·3		CC	–
		UDC	–	–		UDC	15	3·8		UDC	1
		Total		14·1		Total		43·5			
		None	182	85·9		None	226	56·5		None	22
		Total	213	100·0		Total	400	100·0		Total	27
1950	297	CB	18	6·1	315	CB	49	15·6	13	CB	–
		B	15	5·0		B	44	14·0		B	–
		CC	17	5·7		CC	22	7·0		CC	–
		UDC	–	–		UDC	15	4·8		UDC	–
		Total		16·8		Total		41·4			
		None	247	83·2		None	185	58·6		None	13
		Total	297	100·0		Total	315	100·0		Total	13
1951	320	CB	17	5·3	295	CB	43	14·5	10	CB	–
		B	19	6·0		B	42	14·1		B	–
		CC	16	5·0		CC	20	6·8		CC	1
		UDC	1	0·3		UDC	16	5·4		UDC	–
		Total		16·6		Total		40·8			
		None	267	83·4		None	174	59·2		None	9
		Total	320	100·0		Total	295	100·0		Total	10
1955	343	CB	26	7·6	277	CB	38	13·7	10	CB	–
		B	21	6·1		B	37	13·4		B	–
		CC	17	5·0		CC	22	7·9		CC	–
		UDC	7	2·0		UDC	16	5·8		UDC	–
		Total		20·7		Total		40·8			
		None	272	79·3		None	164	59·2		None	10
		Total	343	100·0		Total	277	100·0		Total	10
1959	365	CB	31	8·5	258	CB	31	12·0	7	CB	–
		B	29	7·9		B	34	13·2		B	–
		CC	24	6·6		CC	22	8·5		CC	–
		UDC	9	2·5		UDC	15	5·6		UDC	–
		Total		25·5		Total		39·3			
		None	272	74·5		None	156	60·7		None	7
		Total	365	100·0		Total	258	100·0		Total	7
1964	301	CB	17	5·6	320	CB	44	13·7	9	CB	–
		B	34	11·3		B	52	16·3		B	–
		CC	25	8·3		CC	24	7·6		CC	1
		UDC	6	2·0		UDC	17	5·3		UDC	–
		Total		27·2		Total		42·9			
		None	219	72·8		None	183	57·1		None	8
		Total	301	100·0		Total	320	100·0		Total	9

(Table continued overleaf)

Table 7.2 (continued)

Election	Total MPs	*Conservative* Coun-cil	No. MPs	%	Total MPs	*Labour* Coun-cil	No. MPs	%	Total MPs	*Other* Coun-cil	No. MPs
1966	253	CB	13	5·1	365	CB	52	14·3	12	CB	–
		B	31	12·3		B	64	17·6		B	–
		CC	23	9·1		CC	23	6·3		CC	1
		UDC	6	2·4		UDC	20	5·5		UDC	–
		Total		28·9		Total		43·7			
		None	180	71·1		None	206	56·3		None	11
		Total	253	100·0		Total	365	100·0		Total	12
1970	330	CB	20	6·1	290	CB	39	13·4	10	CB	–
		B	42	12·7		B	49	16·9		B	1
		CC	27	8·2		CC	18	6·2		CC	–
		UDC	10	3·4		UDC	14	4·8		UDC	–
		Total		30·4		Total		41·3			
		None	231	69·6		None	170	58·7		None	9
		Total	330	100·0		Total	290	100·0		Total	10
Feb. 1974	297	CB	16	5·4	301	CB	45	15·0	37	CB	3
		B	43	14·5		B	61	20·3		B	1
		CC	25	8·4		CC	16	5·3		CC	5
		UDC	11	3·7		UDC	18	6·0		UDC	1
		Total		32·0		Total		46·6			
		None	202	68·0		None	161	53·4		None	27
		Total	297	100·0		Total	301	100·0		Total	37
Oct. 1974	277	CB	12	4·3	319	CB	47	14·7	39	CB	3
		B	43	15·5		B	65	20·4		B	2
		CC	23	8·3		CC	16	5·0		CC	4
		UDC	8	2·9		UDC	20	6·3		UDC	1
		Total		31·0		Total		46·4			
		None	191	69·0		None	171	53·6		None	29
		Total	277	100·0		Total	319	100·0		Total	39

Note: CB – County Borough; B – Non-county Borough; CC – County Council; UDC – Urban (or Rural) District Council

Table 7.3

Local government experience of new MPs, by election

Election	Total MPs	Conservative Coun-cil	No. MPs	%	Total MPs	Labour Coun-cil	No. MPs	%	Total MPs	Other Coun-cil	No. MPs
Pre-1945	182	CB	7	3·8	161	CB	25	15·5	21	CB	1
		B	7	3·8		B	18	11·2		B	1
		CC	16	8·8		CC	18	11·2		CC	–
		UDC	–	–		UDC	8	5·0		UDC	1
		Total		16·4		Total		42·9			
		None	152	83·6		None	92	57·1		None	18
		Total	182	100·0		Total	161	100·0		Total	21
1945	74	CB	4	5·4	244	CB	36	14·8	9	CB	–
		B	2	2·7		B	43	17·6		B	2
		CC	2	2·7		CC	17	6·9		CC	–
		UDC	–	–		UDC	7	2·9		UDC	–
		Total		10·8		Total		42·2			
		None	66	89·2		None	141	57·8		None	7
		Total	74	100·0		Total	244	100·0		Total	9
1950	102	CB	9	8·8	62	CB	8	12·9	5	CB	–
		B	9	8·8		B	12	19·4		B	–
		CC	5	4·9		CC	5	8·1		CC	–
		UDC	–	–		UDC	3	4·8		UDC	–
		Total		22·5		Total		45·2			
		None	79	77·5		None	34	54·8		None	5
		Total	102	100·0		Total	62	100·0		Total	5
1951	36	CB	1	2·8	15	CB	2	13·3	2	CB	–
		B	4	11·0		B	2	13·3		B	–
		CC	2	5·5		CC	1	6·7		CC	1
		UDC	1	2·8		UDC	1	6·7		UDC	7
		Total		22·1		Total		40·0			
		None	28	77·9		None	9	60·0		None	1
		Total	36	100·0		Total	15	100·0		Total	2
1955	78	CB	10	12·8	26	CB	4	15·4	2	CB	–
		B	5	6·4		B	6	23·1		B	–
		CC	7	9·0		CC	3	11·5		CC	–
		UDC	6	7·7		UDC	1	3·8		UDC	–
		Total		35·9		Total		53·8			
		None	50	64·1		None	12	46·2		None	2
		Total	78	100·0		Total	26	100·0		Total	2
1959	104	CB	7	6·7	42	CB	3	7·1	1	CB	–
		B	13	12·5		B	7	16·7		B	–
		CC	14	13·5		CC	10	25·8		CC	–
		UDC	4	3·8		UDC	3	7·1		UDC	–
		Total		36·5		Total		54·7			
		None	66	63·5		None	19	45·3		None	1
		Total	104	100·0		Total	42	100·0		Total	1

(Table continued overleaf)

Table 7.3 (continued)

Election	Total MPs	Conservative Coun-cil	No. MPs	%	Total MPs	Labour Coun-cil	No. MPs	%	Total MPs	Other Coun-cil	No. MPs
1964	64	CB	1	1·5	106	CB	18	17·0	6	CB	–
		B	10	15·7		B	24	22·6		B	–
		CC	10	15·7		CC	6	5·7		CC	1
		UDC	1	1·5		UDC	7	6·6		UDC	–
		Total		34·4		Total		51·9			
		None	42	65·6		None	51	48·1		None	5
		Total	64	100·0		Total	106	100·0		Total	6
1966	13	CB	1	7·8	72	CB	12	16·7	5	CB	–
		B	3	23·1		B	15	20·8		B	–
		CC	1	7·8		CC	1	1·4		CC	–
		UDC	–	–		UDC	3	4·2		UDC	–
		Total		38·7		Total		43·1			
		None	8	61·3		None	41	56·9		None	5
		Total	13	100·0		Total	72	100·0		Total	5
1970	92	CB	7	7·6	64	CB	7	10·9	4	CB	–
		B	15	16·3		B	11	17·2		B	1
		CC	4	4·3		CC	1	1·6		CC	–
		UDC	4	4·3		UDC	6	9·4		UDC	–
		Total		32·5		Total		39·1			
		None	62	67·5		None	39	60·9		None	3
		Total	92	100·0		Total	64	100·0		Total	4
Feb. 1974	62	CB	3	4·8	46	CB	8	17·4	21	CB	2
		B	7	11·3		B	13	28·3		B	–
		CC	4	6·5		CC	–	–		CC	4
		UDC	3	4·8		UDC	5	10·8		UDC	1
		Total		27·4		Total		56·5			
		None	45	72·6		None	20	43·5		None	14
		Total	62	100·0		Total	46	100·0		Total	21
Oct. 1974	8	CB	–	–	22	CB	4	18·2	7	CB	–
		B	1	12·5		B	3	13·7		B	1
		CC	1	12·5		CC	1	4·5		CC	–
		UDC	–	–		UDC	2	9·0		UDC	–
		Total		25·0		Total		45·4			
		None	6	75·0		None	12	54·6		None	6
		Total	8	100·0		Total	22	100·0		Total	7

Two reasons may explain why Conservative MPs in the first part of this period were less likely to have entered Parliament after earlier service in local government [5]. Firstly, one of the more popular occupational backgrounds of Conservative MPs, the regular armed forces, was incompatible with membership of a local authority [6]. This did not mean, of course, that there was any legal bar to local council membership (although there was, and is, to membership of Parliament), but rather that the problems of finding the time and being in the correct geographical area effectively prevented such membership. The second reason is that, given a different social outlook, potential Conservative parliamentary candidates tended to aim directly at Parliament rather than first seeking election to a local authority. In recent years, the importance of both factors has declined. There has been a decrease in the number of ex-servicemen MPs (that is, Members who had served in the armed forces other than when conscripted) and, similarly, Conservative candidates are finding it increasingly difficult to be selected to contest initially a safe parliamentary constituency [7]. The result has been that more potential Conservative MPs are finding it necessary to seek election to a local authority before being rewarded with an appropriate parliamentary seat to contest.

It is more difficult to assess the contribution of local politics in the recruitment of MPs in the minor parties. On the surface, it would appear that a municipal background is less important: less than 20 per cent of minor party MPs had previously held an elective office on a local authority. But this conclusion would be misleading in that it does not distinguish between different groups. The Nationalists have, almost without exception, been elected directly to Parliament. Indeed, the absence of local government successes until the recent revival of Nationalist fortunes both nationally and locally has prevented any opportunity for experience in local politics. Liberals, on the other hand, as befits a party which emphasises community politics, have been involved in local government to an extent which is comparable with the two major parties. In fact, parliamentary success for many Liberal candidates has been realised through the progressive extension of a secure local electoral base.

Although no attempt is made here to assess the implications for parliamentary behaviour of this factor in political recruitment, two brief points should perhaps be made. Firstly, it is important to note that in the overwhelming majority of cases the transfer from local to national politics was immediate. Of those Members with a local government background who were returned at the 1970 General Election, for example, 79·1 per cent had been first elected to Parliament whilst actually serving as councillors [8]. Clearly, then, any legacies of their municipal backgrounds would not have been diminished by the passage of time. A second, and probably more significant feature, is that in many cases there was a geographical connection between the ward which they represented on the local authority and the constituency which they represented at Westminster. Again the 1970 figures may be used to illustrate this point. Of the Members returned at that election with a local government background, 41·8 per cent had served on a local authority which had 'direct connections' with the constituency which they represented in Parliament [9]. On this point it is possible to make a distinction between the two major parties. In the Conservative Party, there was a geographical correlation in the case of 24·4 per cent of such Members. The equivalent figure for the Labour Party was 62·7 per cent. Thus nearly two-thirds of Labour Members with local government experience actually represented in Parliament a district which was related to that which they had formerly represented on a local authority [10]. Since residence qualifications are required for membership of a local council, this means that they will, unlike most MPs, live locally. Moreover, there is good reason for believing that, in the Labour Party, earlier service in local government leads to a greater concern with their constituency role after they are elected to Parliament. One study of backbench activity has found that '81·5 per cent of former (Labour) councillors concentrated their activity to some extent on constituency matters' [11].

Throughout the period since 1945 local councils, particularly in London and its surrounding boroughs [12], have proved popular pools from which many successful parliamentary candidates have been recruited. Indeed the figures which have been presented, because of the absence of official biographical data on Members of Parliament, almost certainly err on the side of underestimation. This background of local government service has been especially common among Labour Members of Parliament. During these thirty years, a large and relatively stable proportion of MPs have been returned to the Labour benches at Westminster after previously serving as elected members of a local authority, and there is evidence to suggest that selection committees in Labour's safer constituencies will often give favourable consideration to potential candidates with local government experience. The predominance of ex-councillors amongst sponsored Members of the PLP, who often represent these safe constituencies, illustrates this point. In 1966, for example, 52 per cent of sponsored Labour MPs had previously served on local councils compared with 37·5 per cent of other Labour MPs. A second group amongst whom ex-councillors have been particularly well represented are women Members on both sides of the House. Of the 76 women who won general elections in this period, 33 (43·4 per cent) had earlier served on a local council. This compared with 34·7 per cent of male Members elected during the same period.

Some years ago, P.G. Richards noted that: 'Membership of a local council is regarded as a useful preliminary for a future parliamentarian, and the most forceful of Labour councillors often generate parliamentary ambitions. In the Conservative Party social status is more important than past service' [13]. Certainly there is much evidence that Conservative MPs have been more likely to be active in chambers of commerce, employers' associations, as governors of local schools and colleges, whilst Labour Members have tended to be more involved in the control and conduct of local amenities in general, and of local councils in particular. Biographical information which the parties publish about their candidates, for example, tends to stress local government service in the case of the Labour Party whilst the Conservative Party is more precise about experience and record in other spheres, particularly business and the armed forces. But in both parties local government has now become an important factor in parliamentary recruitment. There is, however, one important qualification to this conclusion. Whilst the practice of recruiting parliamentarians from local activitists, particularly in the North of England, Scottish and Welsh Labour constituencies has remained strong, such MPs rarely achieve leading positions in their parliamentary party. Only two politicians have, during this century, successfully transferred from local to national leadership. These are Neville Chamberlain and Herbert Morrison. Unlike America, local (or state) leadership is not a passport to national leadership. The leading positions in all British parties are occupied by those who have entered national politics at an early age.

The armed forces in Parliament

Unlike local political experience, a service background is very much a Conservative phenomenon. The customary association between the Conservative Party and the defence forces is reflected in the recruitment of Tory MPs. A significant number of Conservative Members are elected to Parliament after a spell of duty in the regular armed forces, most frequently the army [14] and, in contrast to municipal experience in the PLP, a service background is far from rare among those who occupy leading offices in the Conservative Party.

Altogether, 210 MPs (11·9 per cent) have been recruited from the army, navy or air force. This figure includes both those whose sole career prior to election was in one of the three branches of the defence forces and those who, after a brief spell of service, subsequently engaged in a second career before opting for political life. All but seventeen of these ex-service personnel belonged to the Conservative Party, and approximately 25 per cent of Conservative MPs during these thirty years have claim to some experience of regular service life. The service culture in the Conservative Party is also reflected by the numbers attending service colleges (especially Sandhurst). Nearly 10 per cent of Conservatives attended a service college as part of their education.

A review of the strength of this factor in parliamentary recruitment suggests that there has been little change during these thirty years (Figure 7.2). On one hand, there might have been a slight decrease in the proportion of service personnel on Conservative benches, yet there remains the suggestion that constituency parties in areas where Conservatives are dominant, are more favourably disposed to potential candidates with a service background. The impact of this recruitment, no doubt, serves to reinforce Conservative concern with a strong defence policy.

Sponsorship in Parliament

Trade unions have always occupied a central position in the Labour Party. The Parliamentary Labour Party was formed out of a nucleus of trade union MPs and ever since this group has played a crucial role within the PLP. In all selection committees trade unionists are represented, but in some cases unions offer to contribute substantially to electoral expenses if their candidates are nominated. These sponsored candidates account for about one-fifth of all Labour candidates, and about one-third of all Labour MPs. Offers of assistance with expenses help the cause of sponsored candidates and most find nomination in a safe constituency. Of all qualifications available to Labour parliamentary candidates, an offer of sponsorship by a trade union remains the one which is most likely to guarantee electoral success. At these ten elections the success rate of sponsored candidates

(a) All Conservatives

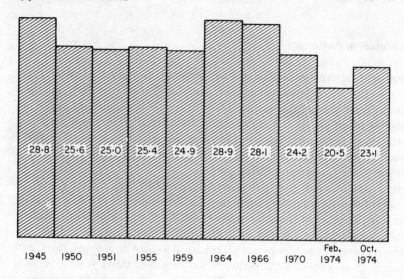

(b) New Conservatives

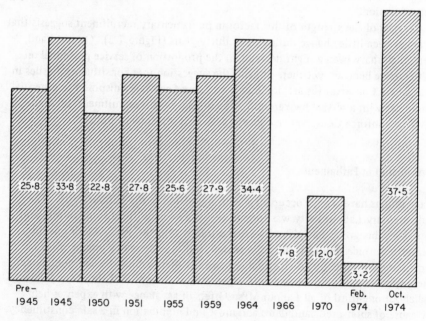

Figure 7.2   Conservative MPs serving in the armed forces (percentages)

has averaged around 75 per cent. In the case of National Union of Mineworkers' candidates, it is nearer 90 per cent. Any study of parliamentary recruitment in Britain would be incomplete without at least some reference to these 'Members from the Unions' [15].

In excess of three-quarters of Labour MPs hold trade union membership cards and a good number of these are active in the trade union movement. It would be an almost impossible task to determine precisely what role all Labour MPs had played in trade union affairs prior to their election, but some indication of this involvement might be gauged from the number who previously held office in a union (Figure 7.3). Obviously these figures represent only those whose official union positions are recorded in the biographical sources which have been used in this study. The actual numbers will no doubt be much greater, but even this limited data suggests considerable and active involvement in trade union affairs amongst a sizeable proportion of Labour MPs.

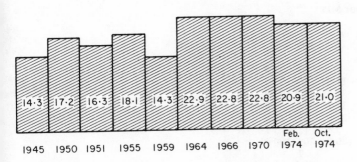

Figure 7.3   Labour MPs occupying official trade union positions (percentages)

In order to examine the social profile and political experience of sponsored MPs, the 1966 group has been selected as a sample intake. This should not be taken to imply that this group is typical of sponsored Members throughout this period: indeed, there have been distinct changes in the composition of this group during these thirty years. Rather, it simply enables some comparisons to be made between the backgrounds of sponsored and non-sponsored MPs in the Labour Party. Nor, incidentally, should the concentration on the Labour Party throughout this section lead to the conclusion that there have been no sponsored MPs on the Conservative benches. In fact, there have been occasional sponsored Conservatives, but only infrequently.

At the 1966 election, 365 Labour MPs were returned. Of these 154 were sponsored by a trade union (or from the Co-operative Party) and 211 unsponsored. Simple comparisons between the sponsored and unsponsored MPs may be made in terms of ease of initial election, incidence of local political experience and age of election (Table 7.4).

101

Table 7.4
Sponsored Labour MPs, 1966

(a) Seats contested prior to first election

Contests	1		2		3		4		5		Nil	
	Spon	Oth	Spon	Oth	Spon	Oth	Spon	Oth	Spon	Oth	Spon	Oth
No. MPs	28	67	20	31	9	5	1	3	–	1	96	104
Per cent	18·2	31·8	13·0	14·7	5·8	2·4	0·7	1·4	–	0·5	62·3	49·2

(b) Local government service

Authority	CB		B		CC		UDC/RDC		None	
	Spon	Oth	Spon	Oth	Spon	Oth	Spon	Oth	Spon	Oth
No. MPs	22	30	32	32	10	13	16	4	74	132
Per cent	14·3	14·2	20·8	15·2	6·5	6·2	10·4	1·9	48·0	62·5

(c) Ages of Labour MPs

	Spon		Oth	
	MPs	%	MPs	%
21–30	–	–	6	2·9
30–39	17	11·0	50	23·9
40–49	48	31·4	50	23·9
50–59	50	32·7	52	24·8
60–69	33	21·6	39	18·8
70+	5	3·3	12	5·7
	154	100·0	209	100·0
INA	1		2	
Average	51·8 years		50·8 years	

The comparison of electoral contests prior to first election shows that sponsored candidates do, in fact, find their initial election to be that much easier than their unsponsored colleagues. In the 1966 sample, 62·3 per cent of the sponsored MPs were successful at their first contest, compared with 49·2 per cent of other Labour Members. Sponsored candidates are more likely to be allocated the safer Labour constituencies and they are also more likely to have served in local government. Referring again to the 1966 figures, 52 per cent of sponsored Members had been active in local politics, compared with 37·5 per cent of unsponsored Labour MPs.

Reference has already been made on a number of occasions in this study, that some form of political apprenticeship is a frequent characteristic in the recruitment of Labour MPs. In the main, it is the sponsored MP who has largely undergone this apprenticeship. One result of this is that sponsored candidates do, on average, tend to seek parliamentary election rather later in life than their unsponsored colleagues. This should not disguise the overall evidence that, like all Labour MPs, those sponsored by trade unions are entering Parliament noticeably younger.

The most revealing characteristics are, of course, educational and occupational backgrounds. Again the 1966 figures are used by way of illustration (Tables 7.5 and 7.6). Before looking at these it is appropriate to recall the purpose of sponsorship as seen by the unions. In crude terms it is to foster in Parliament the interests of the unions and, consequently, the workers represented by these unions. It is interest representation. In choosing people to do this, unions are faced with the choice of either selecting a younger career politician who may achieve front bench status or a senior member of their own union (either from the leadership or rank and file) who will probably remain on the backbenches. The transition in the composition of the Labour Party since 1945 makes plain the fact that leading positions are now won by those who have entered politics early, and with university and professional backgrounds. To an extent, the unions have reflected this change

Table 7.5

Education of sponsored Labour MPs, 1966

	Sponsored MPs	%	Other Labour MPs	%
Elementary only	43	} 46·2	11	} 10·5
Elementary +	28		11	
Secondary only	18		18	
Secondary +	10		3	
Secondary/professional	9		19	
Secondary/university	34	22·1	74	35·4
Secondary/service college	–		–	
Secondary/service/university	–		–	
Private only	–		1	
Private/service college	–		1	
Private/university	–		–	
Private/service/university	–		–	
Private/professional	–		–	
Public only	4		7	
Public/professional	1		3	
Public/service college	–		–	
Public/'Oxbridge'	4	2·6	42	20·1
Public/other university	3		19	
Foreign/UK university	–		–	
Abroad	–		–	
INA	–		2	
Total	154		211	
All public schools	12	7·8	71	34·0
Eton	–		3	
Oxford	7	} 7·8	36	} 27·8
Cambridge	5		22	
London	6	3·9	30	14·4
Wales	3		6	
Scotland	4		16	
Ireland	–		1	
Foreign	1		2	
Other universities	15		22	
All universities	41	26·6	135	64·6

Table 7.6
Occupations of sponsored Labour MPs, 1966

	Sponsored MPs	%	Other Labour MPs	%
Barrister	3	1·9	30	14·4
Solicitor	2		16	
Chartered surveyor/engineer	7		8	
Civil service/local government	1		3	
Services	–		1	
Diplomatic services	–		1	
Lecturer	7		36	
School teacher	10		20	
Doctor/dentist	1		7	
Chartered accountant/secretary	–		5	
Scientific worker	2		2	
Minister of religion	–		–	
Social worker	–		1	
Total (professions)	33	21·5	126	60·3
Small business	–		2	
Director	–		7	
Banker/financier	–		–	
Executive/management	7		7	
Commerce/insurance	–		2	
Business consultant	1		5	
Clerical	2		3	
Total (business)	10	6·5	26	12·4
White collar	6		8	
Political worker	4		1	
Trade union official	35	22·9	2	1·0
Farmer/landowner	–		4	
Housewife	1		3	
Student	–		–	
Journalist/author	7	4·6	31	14·8
Public relations	4		1	
Actor	–		1	
Pilot	–		–	
Policeman	–		–	
Total (miscellaneous)	57	37·0	51	24·4
Railwayman	7		1	
Miner	22		–	
Skilled worker	18		1	
Semi/unskilled worker	7		4	
Total (workers)	54	35·0	6	2·9
INA	0		2	
Grand total	154		211	

in their choice of candidates. But, and this is a vital qualification, some unions (especially the 'blue collar' unions) have retained a preference for the notion of 'actual representation' [16]. In effect, this means representation *of labour* and *by labour.*

This preference for 'actual representation' is reflected in sponsored Members' educational backgrounds. In 1966, of ninety-three MPs who received an elementary education, seventy-eight were sponsored. Thirty-four per cent of unsponsored Labour MPs attended public school, compared with 7·8 per cent of sponsored Members. Of unsponsored Labour Members 64·6 per cent attended university, compared with 26·6 per cent of sponsored MPs.

The contrast in occupational terms is even more striking. In 1966, of the sixty ex-manual workers on the Labour benches, only six were unsponsored. Without its sponsored MPs, the PLP loses virtually all of its ex-worker Members. For a party which relies so heavily on its share of the workers' vote and is so historically and ideologically connected with this section of the community, this is extremely important.

In terms of recruitment, the most fundamental contribution of sponsorship is clearly that it brings into Parliament members of the working classes. Indeed, it now appears that the only practicable way open to a potential Member from these classes is adoption by, and consequent financial assistance from, a trade union. Traditionally, most unions have shown some preference for people of their own kind, be they officials or rank and file. Symbolic connections are important in all branches of political activity and for some unionists merely getting their own kind into Parliament is a sufficient end in itself. Emphasis on social origins is especially strong in certain unions, of which the National Union of Mineworkers (NUM) is a classic example. This union has proved consistent in sponsoring its own kind as parliamentary candidates. Typically, they are either miners or NUM officials and are first elected in their late forties or early fifties [17]. Of all unions, it also probably exercises greatest influence over its sponsored MPs.

Separating these two elements within the Labour Party emphasises the process of embourgeoisement in the PLP. But it would be a mistake to assume that the trade union group of MPs have remained untouched by this process. Although perhaps to a lesser degree than their unsponsored colleagues, they too have changed in their social profile. Whilst some unions (notably the National Union of Mineworkers and the National Union of Railwaymen) cling to the ideal of sending their own kind to Westminster, other large unions have increasingly sponsored middle class recruits. The Transport and General Workers' Union and the National Union of General and Municipal Workers, for example, have for a number of years now sponsored predominantly young, graduate, professional candidates [18]. This penetration by middle class men from the unions has been particularly marked in urban seats.

Not unexpectedly, the vital relationship between the Labour Party and the trade unions is weakened by these changes. The sponsorship of career parliamentarians with more tenuous links with their sponsoring unions is unlikely to cement the party/union relationship. At the same time, the political positions of the sponsored MPs has shifted noticeably. On the basis of an analysis of Early Day Motions, Berrington has argued that there has been a pronounced move towards left-wing views among trade union MPs [19]. In the first decade of this study, the trade union sponsored MPs predominantly supported the Right. With each cohort from 1959, they adopt markedly less moderate positions. They are now better represented in the Tribune Group than on the backbenches as a whole, and this drift away from 'actual representation' shows every sign of continuing. There can be little doubt that some direct representatives of manual workers will continue to be recruited as a result of sponsorship, but the fact cannot be denied that without sponsorship, the Labour Party loses virtually all of its actual *labour* in Parliament and even this group is being weakened by unions selecting more career politicians to sponsor.

Women in Parliament

Considering the intensity with which women campaigned for an equal franchise in the early part of this century, their electoral successes since 1918, when they achieved the right to sit in the House of Commons [20], have been remarkably rare. The year 1975 was International Women's Year and by this time there had been considerable advances in the position of women. The statute book now contains laws forbidding sex discrimination, ensuring equal pay for women workers in most occupations and more favourable divorce settlements. Moreover, a woman now leads one of the two major political parties and, for the last decade or so, it has been customary for both Conservative and Labour parties to include one or two women on their Front Bench. Despite this, the representation of women in our elected legislature remains, as it does in almost all other countries, extremely poor. Of all socio-economic groups, women are the most under-represented at Westminster.

The first woman to successfully contest a general election was Constance Markievicz in 1918 but, being a Sinn Fein member, she failed to take her seat. Nancy Astor, a Conservative, was the first woman to actually take her place in the House, following her by-election success at Plymouth, Sutton in November 1919. She was joined by a second woman MP after the 1922 General Election. In the inter-war years, there was a slow rise in their numbers reaching its peak in 1931 when fifteen women were returned to the House of Commons. Altogether between 1918 and 1945, thirty-eight women were elected (Table 7.7).

At the ten general elections since 1945, a further seventy-six women have found their way to Westminster. The actual number of women MPs after any election has fluctuated between seventeen and twenty-nine. Thus, even at their most successful election in 1964, less than one MP in twenty was a woman.

It is interesting to consider why women are so badly represented in Parliament [21]. Certainly the under-representation of the female half of the population is by

Table 7.7
Election of women MPs

(a) All MPs

	1945	1950	1951	1955	1959	1964	1966	1970	Feb. 1974	Oct. 1974
Conservative	1	6	6	10	12	11	7	15	9	7
Labour	21	14	11	14	13	18	19	10	13	18
Other	2	1	–	–	–	–	–	1	1	2
Total	24	21	17	24	25	29	26	26	23	27

(b) New MPs

	Pre- 1945	1945	1950	1951	1955	1959	1964	1966	1970	Feb. 1974	Oct. 1974
Conservative	3	–	3	–	4	5	1	1	7	1	–
Labour	6	15	4	–	3	1	5	2	1	4	5
Other	2	–	–	–	–	–	–	–	1	1	1
Total	11	15	7	0	7	6	6	3	9	6	6

no means limited to Britain. In the French Assembly the proportion of females in recent years averages 2 per cent. In Canada and USA it is also 2 per cent, and 5 per cent in New Zealand. In comparison, in Sweden and Finland women fare significantly better and account for approximately 22 per cent of the national legislatures. In Britain since 1945, women have only provided a fairly consistent 4 per cent of our elected politicians.

One obvious factor which places women at a disadvantage are their traditional family responsibilities. All the British political parties show a preference for married over single women as candidates [22] and this naturally makes it that much more difficult for such women to find the time and the means to establish their claims for party nomination. Even if they are able to overcome this hurdle, they are then faced with the problem, if elected, of combining married and family life with parliamentary life away in London. The conventional socialisation of women has reinforced the idea of woman's family responsibilities. It is that much easier, therefore, for the politically motivated woman to engage in local rather than national politics since it imposes less demands in terms of time and travelling. Approximately three times the proportion of women in national politics are engaged in local politics [23]. Whatever the cause, the most important reason why there are so few women MPs is their own failure to put themselves forward as candidates [24]. The way in which women's largest organisation, the Women's Institute, itself steered clear of political issues until very recently is a nice reflection of this reticence.

This is not to say that women play only a small part in British party politics: as a group, they almost certainly provide over half the membership of the Conservative Party and very large proportions of the membership of the Labour, Liberal and Nationalist parties. And the parties themselves have made efforts to get more female parliamentary candidates. Conservative Central Office has frequently reminded constituencies that it views the small number of female candidates with some dissatisfaction and has urged them to include more women on their short-lists. Such pleas have met with little actual success and of the seventy-six women MPs in this period, only twenty-five were Conservatives. Women have fared a little better in the Labour Party, having forty-six of their sex returned in these thirty years. Indeed, women in the Labour Party have five seats reserved for them on the National Executive Committee. Perhaps not surprisingly, it is in the Liberal and minor parties that the largest proportions of women candidates emerge. It is now normal practice in the Liberal Party for constituency selection committees to consider at least one woman on their short-lists. And not only are two of the eleven SNP Members women, it was the by-election success of a woman, Mrs W. Ewing at Hamilton in 1967, which signalled the rise in the fortunes of the Scottish National Party.

Although the main cause of the under-representation of women appears to be their own failure to present themselves as candidates [25], and despite the encouragement of party central offices to foster more women volunteers, the evidence does suggest that where women come forward, the main political parties [26] do discriminate against them when selecting candidates for their better seats. Ross came to the conclusion that an 'abnormal proportion of . . . hopeless struggles . . . have fallen to the lot of women, in comparison with the number of safe seats or even borderline constituencies, for which they have been adopted' [27]. Indeed, he formulated the theory that women have an electoral handicap factor of 2, that is their chances of success, even after securing nomination, are half as good as that of the average man [28]. A more recent review of discrimination in selecting for safe seats came to similar conclusions. In the February 1974 election, women were adopted in 3 per cent of the better Conservative seats, 4·3 per cent of the better Labour seats and 3·8 per cent of the better Liberal seats [29]. By contrast the proportion of women in the worse seats were 7·4 per cent, 8·4 per cent and 9·5 per cent respectively. Thus whilst there is no evidence to suggest that the electorate, when voting, show any disfavour to female candidates [30], there remains what has been described as the 'suspicions and reservations and prejudice of the selectorate' who actually choose parliamentary contenders [31].

The difficulties facing potential women candidates is reflected in the electoral experiences of those who actually arrived at Westminster (Table 7.8). In this period, 59·9 per cent of all male Members were elected at their first contest. Among women MPs the equivalent figure is 54 per cent, and the range of those who needed more than one contest suggests that more subsequent attempts were necessary for women than men. Again, it should be pointed out that the performance of women in the minor parties is rather unusual and cannot be compared with the performance of Conservative and Labour women. All five minor party women MPs were elected at their first attempt.

In terms of age at the time of their first election, women also differ slightly from their male colleagues (Table 7.9). Although the gap in average ages is only slight,

Table 7.8
Women MPs contesting seats before first election

No. of contests	Con	Lab	Oth	Total	Per cent	Male MPs
1	4	13	–	17	22·4	(23·4)
2	5	4	–	9	11·8	(12·3)
3	2	2	–	4	5·3	(3·4)
4	–	3	–	3	3·9	(0·7)
5	1	1	–	2	2·6	(0·3)
Total	12	23	–	35	46·0	(40·1)
Nil	13	23	5	41	54·0	(59·9)
Total	25	46	5	76	100·0	(100·0)

Table 7.9
Age of female and male MPs, on the occasion of their first election (percentages)

Age	Conservative Male	Female	Labour Male	Female	Total (inc. Oth) Male	Female
21–29	8·6	–	4·4	8·8	6·5	10·0
30–39	42·1	40·9	31·9	35·2	37·2	36·7
40–49	35·4	40·9	40·9	26·5	37·9	30·0
50–59	12·0	13·6	18·4	26·5	15·0	20·0
60–69	1·8	4·6	4·3	3·0	3·3	3·3
70+	0·1	–	0·1	–	0·1	–
Total	100·0	100·0	100·0	100·0	100·0	100·0
Average age	40·5 years	42·8 years	42·4 years	43·3 years	41·5 years	43·0 years

43 years in the case of women and 41·5 years for men, the distribution of ages suggests a greater likelihood of entry to Parliament after the age of forty. In general, this implies a preference for more experienced candidates and, in particular, that selection committees will need to be satisfied that a woman's domestic responsibilities have passed their peak before adopting her as a parliamentary candidate. Women themselves will be more likely to generate parliamentary ambitions after their family responsibilities, especially to young children, have lessened. A concomitant of this, of course, is that later entry will also limit the length of their parliamentary careers. As a result, the length of the parliamentary service of women MPs has usually been less than that of their male colleagues [32].

A similar contrast emerges regarding local government experience (Table 7.10). Of male MPs 34·7 per cent had previously served in local government, compared with 43·4 per cent of women. The difference between the sexes in the

Table 7.10
Women MPs with local government experience

Type of Council	Con	Lab	Oth	Total	Per cent	Male MPs
County Borough	4	6	1	11	14·5	(10·0)
Borough	4	5	–	9	11·8	(13·4)
County council	3	5	–	8	10·5	(7·6)
Urban/rural district	1	4	–	5	6·6	(3·7)
Total	12	20	1	33	43·4	(34·7)
None	13	26	4	43	56·6	(65·3)
Total	25	46	5	76	100·0	(100·0)

Conservative Party on this point is especially notable. Whilst only a quarter of Conservative men had a municipal background, almost one half of women in this party were recruited from local politics. The minor parties excepted, local government service is an important influence in furthering political ambitions among women. With party activism and voluntary work as lesser influences, it ranks as probably 'the most significant pre-election experience' [33].

Conservative women in this period largely followed a similar educational route to their male colleagues (Table 7.11). Obviously there are so few women members that it is difficult to formulate any instructive hypotheses, although it is perhaps worth noting that the public school element [34] is slightly smaller than it is amongst male Conservative Members and that the proportion of women graduates was one-third, compared with the two-thirds male graduates. Women Labour Members were, for the most part, educated in secondary schools. Approximately the same proportion of women as men received their education in an elementary school, but the proportion of women who attended secondary school was larger. Particularly large was the proportion of secondary school/university educated women Members. One-third of all Labour women had this educational background. The secondary school/professional route was also popular. Both of these educational backgrounds relate to the preponderance of women teachers, lecturers and journalists. Thus, the most prominent features of the educational backgrounds of women MPs have been the large proportion who received a secondary education and the relatively small proportion who were educated at a public school.

The social composition of the group of women MPs is perhaps best revealed by their occupational backgrounds (Table 7.12). Immediately apparent, is the fact that working class women are almost wholly excluded from election. No woman was primarily engaged in manual work and the very few recruits from this section of the community (Mrs E. Braddock being the most notable) owe their election to trade union involvement and even with the unions, their opportunities are restricted by the fact that the unions with the strongest parliamentary representation operate in traditionally male-dominated industries. Business is better represented by women, but still to a lesser degree than among their male colleagues. Quite a few are journalists and a similar number describe themselves as housewives but the most

Table 7.11

Table 7.11
Education of female and male Members

	Con		Lab		Oth		Total			
	Men	Wo-men	Men	Wo-men	Men	Wo-men	Men	%	Wo-men	%
Elementary only	5	1	166	7	2	–	173 } 16·2		8 } 14·3	
Elementary +	1	1	93	1	1	–	95		2	
Secondary only	41	2	83	4	10	–	134		6	
Secondary +	–	–	32	1	1	–	33		1	
Secondary/professional	18	1	61	7	7	–	86		8	
Secondary/university	69	4	216	15	20	4	305	18·5	23	32·9
Secondary/service college	–	–	–	–	1	–	1		–	
Secondary/service/univ.	1	–	–	–	–	–	1		2	
Private only	8	2	2	–	1	–	11			
Private/service college	13	–	1	–	–	–	14		–	
Private/university	5	–	–	–	–	–	5		–	
Private/service/university	3	–	–	–	1	–	4		–	
Private/professional	1	–	1	–	–	–	2		–	
Public only	105	6	18	1	6	–	129		7	
Public/professional	38	1	5	2	2	–	45		3	
Public/service college	48	–	2	–	–	–	50		–	
Public/'Oxbridge'	370	2	83	4	15	–	468	28·4	6	8·6
Public/other university	46	3	38	1	7	–	91		4	
Foreign/UK university	–	–	2	–	–	–	2		–	
Abroad	1	–	–	–	–	–	1		–	
INA	17	2	11	3	4	1	32		6	
Total	790	25	814	46	78	5	1682		76	
All public schools	607	12	146	8	30	–	783	47·5	20	28·6
Eton	165	–	8	–	2	–	175		–	
Oxford	222	3	85	5	11	–	318 } 33·0		8 } 22·9	
Cambridge	179	1	40	7	8	–	227		8	
London	22	2	72	3	1	–	95		5	
Wales	5	–	25	–	7	–	37		–	
Scotland	19	–	41	2	12	2	72		4	
Ireland	9	2	3	–	1	1	13		3	
Foreign	9	–	7	–	–	–	16		–	
Other universities	29	1	66	3	3	1	98		5	
All universities	494	9	339	20	43	4	876	53·1	33	47·1

common area of recruitment is from the professions, especially teaching. Over a quarter of women MPs were previously engaged in this occupation.

With such a small sample, it is difficult to detect any changes in the pattern of female representation, but clearly there is little to suggest that, Nationalist parties apart, women have made any progress since 1945. Their under-representation derives, for the most part, from their failure, whatever the cause, to beget political ambitions. There is some discrimination in the allocation of better seats, but the main cure for the anomalous position of women must be the awakening of their own political awareness and ambitions. Other remedies, such as reformed voting systems, can only play a minor part [35]. It is a matter of conjecture how far the considerable exclusion of women from our legislature has contributed to the grievances which have figured in much of the literature of women's movements.

Table 7.12
Occupation of female and male Members

	Con Men	Con Women	Lab Men	Lab Women	Oth Men	Oth Women	Total Men	Total %	Total Women	Total %
Barrister	132	3	65	–	8	–	205	12·3	3	4·4
Solicitor	25	–	32	–	4	1	61		1	
Ch. surveyor/engineer	17	–	24	–	3	–	44		–	
Civil service/local govt.	5	–	12	1	–	–	17		1	
Services	59	–	3	–	–	–	62		–	
Diplomatic services	28	–	3	–	1	–	32			
Lecturer	8	–	87	4	4	1	99 }		5 }	
School teacher	8	2	61	10	6	1	75 } 10·4		13 } 26·5	
Doctor/dentist	11	–	17	2	3	–	31		2	
Ch.accountant/secretary	21	–	9	–	3	–	33		–	
Scientific worker	1	–	7	–	–	–	8		–	
Minister of religion	2	–	5	–	2	–	9		–	
Social worker	1	3	1	2	–	–	2		5	
Total (professions)	318	8	326	19	34	3	678	40·6	30	44·1
Small business	2	–	7	–	2	–	11		–	
Director	240	5	21	–	7	–	268	16·1	5	7·4
Banker/financier	18	–	1	–	–	–	19		–	
Executive/management	23	–	27	1	–	–	50		1	
Commerce/insurance	34	–	3	–	2	–	39		–	
Business consultant	13	–	10	–	3	–	26		–	
Clerical	–	1	11	–	–	–	11		1	
Total (business)	330	6	80	1	14	0	424	25·4	7	10·3
White collar	2	–	34	1	2	–	38		1	
Political worker	9	–	11	2	1	–	21		2	
Trade union official	–	–	96	2	–	–	96	5·6	2	2·9
Farmer/landowner	80	2	7	–	15	–	102	6·1	2	2·9
Housewife	–	3	–	7	–	–	–		10	14·7
Student	5	–	–	–	–	1	5		1	
Journalist/author	33	1	60	9	9	1	102	6·1	11	16·2
Public relations	7	1	10	1	–	–	17		2	
Actor	–	–	1	–	–	–	1		–	
Pilot	1	–	–	–	–	–	1		–	
Policeman	–	–	1	–	–	–	1		–	
Total (miscellaneous)	137	7	220	22	27	2	384	23·0	31	45·6
Railwayman	–	–	35	–	–	–	35		–	
Miner	–	–	62	–	–	–	62	–	–	
Skilled worker	1	–	53	–	1	–	55		–	
Semi/unskilled worker	–	–	29	–	1	–	30		–	
Total (workers)	1	0	179	0	2	0	182	11·0	0	0·0
INA	4	4	9	4	1	0	14		8	
Grand total	790	25	814	46	78	5	1682		76	

Notes

[1] Over the years the influence of local government in the House of Commons has been discussed in a number of articles with this title in the journal *Public Administration*: W.J.M. Mackenzie, 1951 and 1954 volumes; David Butler, 1953; Bryan Keith-Lucas, 1955; Colin Mellors, 1974. I am grateful to the Editor of Public Administration for permission to reproduce an amended version of the latter article here.

[2] See, for example, G.W. Jones, *Borough Politics*, Macmillan, London, 1969, p. 160; and A.M. Rees and T. Smith, *Town Councillors*, Acton Society Trust, London, 1964; pp. 72—4.

[3] These calculations are based upon the total length of council service prior to entering Parliament (many Members had served on two councils concurrently, but such service has not been double counted). Such figures were available for slightly over 80 per cent of these MPs in 1974. In the period as a whole, where the length of service of approximately two-thirds of councillor-MPs was discovered, the average length of service prior to entering Parliament was: Labour — 10·5 years; Conservative — 6·9 years.

[4] W.J.M. Mackenzie, 'Conventions of Local Government', *Public Administration*, 1954.

[5] J.F.S. Ross, *Elections and Electors*, Eyre and Spottiswoode, London, 1955, p. 451.

[6] In 1950, for example, 25·6 per cent of Conservative Members had been ex-servicemen.

[7] Of Conservatives returned to Parliament in 1945 86·3 per cent had been elected at their first attempt. By October, 1974, this figure had fallen to 36·7 per cent.

[8] There is little difference between the parties on this point: 83·8 per cent of such Labour Members were elected immediately to Parliament compared with 75 per cent of similar Conservatives.

[9] Direct connection is defined as 'membership of a local authority within the constituency, or within which the constituency lies' (Michael Rush, *The Selection of Parliamentary Candidates*, Nelson, London, 1969, p. 288). Where a Member has represented more than one constituency, only his first has been compared with the area of his local government service. These figures may be compared with those presented by Rush, op. cit., pp. 73—80 (especially Table 3(5)) and Chapter 8; and A. Ranney, *Pathways to Parliament*, Macmillan, London, 1965, pp. 107—13.

[10] Certain areas are also well known for their tendency to choose candidates with strong local connections. In 1970, for example, ten of the fifteen Members returned for Glasgow had previously been members of the City Council.

[11] D. Judge, 'Backbench Specialisation: A Study in Parliamentary Questions', *Parliamentary Affairs*, vol. 27, 1973—4, p. 183.

[12] Of the ex-local government representatives who were returned to Parliament in October 1974, 32 per cent had served on an authority within the area now covered by the GLC. There is little difference between the parties on this point: Labour − 33·3 per cent; Conservatives − 30·8 per cent.

[13] P.G. Richards, *Honourable Members*, Faber, London, 1st ed., 1959, p. 32.

[14] Throughout this section, MPs with a 'service background' are defined as those Members who have served in any of the armed forces at times other than when conscripted.

[15] For a discussion of the role played by the trade unions in the PLP, see J. Ellis and R.W. Johnson, *Members from the Unions*, Fabian Research Series 316, 1974 and M. Harrison, *Trade Unions and the Labour Party since 1945*, Allen and Unwin, London, 1960.

[16] Ellis and Johnson, op. cit., pp. 2−3.

[17] Two current Labour Cabinet Members, Roy Mason and Eric Varley first elected at the ages of 29 and 32 respectively, are notable exceptions to this rule.

[18] Ellis and Johnson, op. cit., pp. 4−14.

[19] J. Leece and H.B. Berrington, 'Backbench Attitudes and Guttman Scaling: A Pilot Study' (unpublished paper). See also, H.B. Berrington, *Backbench Opinion in the House of Commons 1945−55*, Pergamon, London, 1973, p. 192.

[20] Women were finally enfranchised on the same terms as men in 1928.

[21] The rise of women's movements in recent years has led to a number of studies which have focused upon their place in the political arena. J.F.S. Ross devotes a chapter to them in *Electors and Elections*. For a fuller picture, see: M. Currell, *Political Woman*, Croom Helm, London, 1974 and P. Brookes, *Women at Westminster*, Peter Davies, London, 1967. Two short notes concerned specifically with their electoral fortunes are E. Lakeman, 'Political Women in their Year', *Representation*, vol. 15, no. 60, 1975, and M.J. Le Lohe, 'Sex Discrimination and Under-Representation of Women in Politics', *New Community*, Summer 1976.

[22] Rush, op. cit., p. 64.

[23] M.J. Le Lohe, op cit., and *Committee on the Management of Local Government*, vol. 2, 'The Local Government Councillor', HMSO, London, 1967.

[24] Rush, op. cit., pp. 222−3.

[25] Party lists of potential candidates contain relatively few women. See Rush, op cit., p. 63 and p. 223.

[26] Given the peculiar position of the Nationalist parties, no statistical evidence is available as to whether they also appear to favour male candidates in their better seats, but clearly the proportionately larger number of successful women candidates suggests that there is less discrimination.

[27] Ross, op. cit., p. 266.

[28] Ibid., p. 259. This is based on the equation: (women candidates x men Members)÷(women Members x men candidates).

[29] M.J. Le Lohe, op. cit., p. 119. Better Conservative and Labour seats are defined as those which they won and better Liberal seats as those in which their candidate came either first or second.

[30] The proximity of the two 1974 elections was a rare opportunity to compare voting behaviour and Michael Steed found no discrimination was shown by the electorate towards female Conservative and Labour candidates, but some evidence of such a practice in the case of female Liberal candidates, D. Butler and D. Kavanagh, *The British General Election of October 1974*, Macmillan, London, 1975, Appendix 2, p. 345.

[31] P. Paterson, *The Selectorate*, MacGibbon and Kee, London, 1967, p. 45.

[32] Although there have been exceptions, for example, the four Labour women MPs: B. Castle (1945–74), E. Braddock (1945–70), J. Lee (1929–31, 1945–70) and A. Bacon (1945–70). On the Conservative side there has been the unparalleled service of Dame Irene Ward (1931–45, 1950–74).

[33] Currell, op. cit., p. 69.

[34] It is worth recalling at this point that a public school for girls is defined in this study as one of the Principal Girls' Schools (usually fee-paying) listed in *Whitaker's Almanack*.

[35] See Lakeman, op. cit., and Currell, op. cit., p. 179.

8 The profession of politics since 1945 – a reappraisal

The facts are indisputable, but the interpretation to be put upon them seems purely subjective . . . [1]

In the ten general elections which have been held since 1945 some 1,758 Members have been returned to the British House of Commons. Nominally, anyone over twenty-one can become a Member of Parliament, except for aliens, non-dissenting clergy, lunatics, judges, employed civil servants, peers, felons and candidates found guilty of corrupt practices at elections. In practice the reservoir from which parliamentarians are recruited is small and often exclusive. The limited sources of political activists has been noted in other contexts, notably in the recruitment of local government councillors [2]. Even the emergence of new Nationalist MPs in the Commons has failed to bring attendant changes in demographic characteristics. Whatever else it may have been, the House of Commons since 1945 has been anything but a microcosm of the nation.

Without doubt, the most dramatic changes in recruitment patterns have occurred in the Parliamentary Labour Party, where there has been a massive shift away from the working class and towards the middle class. This process of embourgeoisement has steadily progressed throughout this period and within this time-span the size of the Labour manual worker group has been reduced by more than half. Moreover, the claims which workers often had to the better Labour seats has been much less apparent in recent years. This is explained by many trade unions switching away from the idea of 'actual representation' and sponsoring instead articulate career parliamentarians. Only a couple or so of the unions now retain a strong preference for promoting their own men, notably the NUM, and it is the support of these unions which accounts for almost all the remaining workers on the Labour benches at Westminster. The displacement of Labour's men of toil by their men of ideas and rhetoric has been both rapid and unceasing.

In contrast to Labour's shifting and diverse profile, Conservative recruitment remains relatively stable and homogeneous. There has certainly been movement away from the landed and towards business occupations, but not to such an extent as to disturb the overall symmetry of this party at Westminster. The Conservative Party remains the party of breeding and attainment and where one of these two attributes is missing strength in the other may help compensate.

The narrowing of the social base from which the parliamentary parties are recruited (rapid in Labour, gradual and more protracted in the Conservative Party) is common to other Western democracies. Guttsman has observed a similar development in Germany [3]. In the Conservative Party, the decline of the great political families and the loss of a number of aristocratic connections contributes to this apparent further convergence of the political recruitment base. The process has been likened to unisex hairstyles and clothing. 'Nowadays, like the sexes, Labour and Tory backbenchers look much the same from behind' [4], but the inference here is that from the front certain distinctive features help us distinguish male from female. In the same way, despite their apparent resemblance, there are important differences in Conservative and Labour recruitment profiles. The existence in the Conservative Party of exclusive educational backgrounds is one obvious cause of differentiation. Another is the relative homogeneity of that party compared with the diversity of the PLP. The Labour Party remains an amalgam of three distinct elements – established professions, the new (and meritocratic) professions and the rump of manual workers. What has happened over these thirty years is that the balance has tilted away from the workers towards the new professions. What has not happened is the emergence of any new socio-economic groups in Parliament. The lower middle class, clerical and white-collar workers and, increasingly, manual trades are sadly under-represented at Westminster. This distorted pattern of representation must have implications for the conduct of parliamentary politics and we may consider these under several headings: the relationship between Parliament and the electorate; upon the Conservative Party; upon the Labour Party and upon the nature and conduct of parliamentary politics.

Parliament and the electorate

Much of the earlier work on recruitment studies was undertaken by those whose liberal view of the constitution persuaded them of the desirability of MPs being typical of their electors. A.H. Birch has explained this in terms of a neo-Benthamite culture whereby 'legislators, in the process of promoting their own interests and happiness, would automatically maximize the happiness of the population as a whole' [5]. Although primarily used now as a criterion for criticism of Parliament's composition, occasional arguments for more socially equitable political recruitment may be heard. The concern here is with the distribution of power in society. On the other side, there are those who argue for the need to recruit more able and resourceful people to Parliament. The concern here is with the effective functioning of parliamentary leadership. According to the Whig theory of representation MPs are neither delegates nor symbolic representatives, instead, they are elected to promote the interests of the nation as a whole which is determined by their own judgement. These divergent approaches are, therefore, explained by two distinct views about the role and purpose of Parliament itself. The former views the House of Commons as a deliberative assembly which is the collective voice of the electorate, whilst the latter emphasises more the leadership role of Parliament. But even allowing for these differing interpretations, the grossly exaggerated representation of some groups and the virtual absence of others seems unlikely to be the most effective prescription for good parliamentary government.

In this study, the demographic data of all MPs – backbench and front-bench –

have been recorded. The characteristics of those holding government office have not been recorded separately. The reason for this is not primarily methodological convenience, but as an *a priori* assumption about the role of the British House of Commons. There is much misunderstanding about the nature and role of the Commons and a good number of the criticisms levelled against it are misplaced in so far as they envisage for Parliament powers which it has never had. In reality, a primary purpose of Parliament is to legitimise the activities of Governments. Parliament as such fuses government and people. Bagehot describes one function of the House as 'an expressive function. It is its office to express the mind of the English people on all matters which come before it' [6]. To do this, although it need not be the direct spokesman of all our interests, it does need to mobilise the consent of *all* the people. And it is difficult to see how it can effectively do this when its membership virtually excludes vast sections of the community. As it is a political life is a minority taste appealing only to a particular kind of person. The groups who are excluded from Parliament's membership have come to frequently by-pass Westminster and seek direct consultation with Whitehall. This may be especially true of the trade unions. Governments themselves contribute to this by increasingly asking for direct endorsements of their policies (especially in the field of economic policy) instead of operating through Parliament. The consequent decline of the 'traditional consent model' of parliamentary government has led one observer to speak of the replacement of delegatory democracy by participatory democracy [7]. Of course, there are many other factors which have led to a weakening of Parliament's place in our system of government, but clearly the exclusion of some groups is likely to lead them to search for alternative channels to influence Government policies. The effects of weak representation may be seen by two brief illustrations.

Of all social groups women have fared least well in the recruitment of MPs: although they comprise about half the population, less than one MP in twenty is female. Women have, of course, long complained about the discriminatory treatment which they have received in our society, and it seems not unreasonable to infer that some responsibility for this rests with their poor representation in our legislature. Over the past decade, the questions of abortion and divorce law reform have been recurrent concerns in the Commons and in legislating on both, it seems rather inappropriate that the decisions should be taken by a forum primarily composed of men. This is not to say that the woman's viewpoint on these questions should be the only one considered, or is even necessarily different from that of men, but it is less than satisfactory that the opportunities for women to participate in issues which affect them most are so restricted. Nor, incidentally, should it be assumed that the contributions of those women who have managed to be elected to the Commons have been limited to matters affecting their own sex [8].

The second, and rather different, group are the small businessmen. Collectively, small businessmen (manufacturers, retailers, motor trades, construction, catering, etc.) make a considerable contribution to economic and business life [9]. Naturally there are practical difficulties in the way of people from this sector who may wish to seek elective office and only a handful have found their way to Westminster during this period. Like women, they have also felt that they have suffered discriminatory treatment by Governments in recent years. Financial and labour problems have been particular areas of concern [10]. The abolition of Resale Price Maintenance, Value Added Tax and the period of Selective Employment Tax have been frequent complaints. In 1977, their problems were recognised by the appointment of a minister with responsibilities for small firms and the announcement of an inquiry into the operation of small businesses [11], but prior to this, their weak position in Parliament tended to match a weak industrial position. This is especially apparent if they are compared with the farming industry. As voters, farmers are much less numerous than small businessmen (or, indeed, than the agricultural lobby in Italy, Ireland, Australia and the United States), but Parliament itself has been plentiful in farmers and landowners. The farming lobby has thus been strengthened by its parliamentary influence and throughout this period (especially since the 1947 Agriculture Act) the farming industry has received preferential treatment by Governments of both parties [12]. Needless to say, this is not to deny that strategic and other considerations were the strongest motivations in shaping post-war agricultural policies, but the strength of the farming groups in Parliament has been helpful to the cause of the farmers. This contrasts sharply with the position of small businessmen.

The importance of élite – electorate social comparisons, therefore, lies not so much with the distortion of representation, which is a universal phenomenon, but the nature and size of the excluded groups. Concern over declining working class involvement in traditional politics is, of course, prominent in many recent studies [13]. But equally, it seems not unreasonable to contemplate how far apparently wider disaffection with parliamentary politics and government [14] is compounded by a narrowing of the social base from which British MPs are drawn. A common theme in the study of liberal democracies over the last couple of years is the notion of 'overloaded' government. In simple terms, the diagnosis of the problems of governing liberal democracies is expressed in terms of extended expectations by the electorate and complex and economically unviable aspirations of governments [15]. And where governments, not surprisingly, fail to achieve their goals in such circumstances, the failure is as much a failure to bridge the gap between reality and expectations as it is the failure of actual policies. Anything, therefore, which helps foster closer links and better understanding between electors and elected is to be welcomed. It seems rather paradoxical that at the very time that proposals to extend industrial democracy by opening boardroom decision-making to shop-floor representatives are being made [16], the workers are rapidly being displaced from Westminster. The Commons' primary functions as a deliberative and legitimising forum, a process of institutionalised consent, are unlikely to be enhanced by its narrowing recruitment base. The electorate themselves, as reflected in their voting and general attitudes towards Parliament, have been singularly unimpressed by efforts to improve the qualities, and therefore the social exclusiveness, of our parliamentarians.

Conservatives: homogeneity and the dissipation of conflict

A basic strength of the Conservative Party at Westminster is the lack of permanent factions within their parliamentary party. This is not to say that there are no groupings or conflict [17], but what rebellions and splits do appear tend to take the appearance of temporary and *ad hoc* alliances rather than deep-rooted and ideological factions [18]. Essentially, this is explained by the different nature and origins of the two major parties. The Conservative Party has developed over a long period out of various parliamentary groupings, whilst the Labour Party developed from a coalition of extra-parliamentary sources. Nevertheless, the social homogeneity of the Conservative Party in Parliament (and especially between leadership and backbenches) serves to dissipate conflict whilst social cleavages within the PLP fuel existing schisms.

In its electoral support, the Conservative Party receives approximately forty per cent of its votes from the working class and sixty per cent from the middle and upper classes, and this pattern of support has remained stable throughout the last decade [19]. Stability of electoral support is further reflected in greater agreement with Conservative policies amongst Conservative voters than there is apparently by Labour voters for Labour policies [20]. The incongruence between the social composition of Conservative electoral support and Conservative political recruitment does not, therefore, seem to produce any important cleavages. Inside Parliament there is no gulf between the social origins the party's leaders and backbenchers.

Attempts to correlate social backgrounds with issue preferences in this party have produced negative findings [21]. That is to say, attitudinal positions rarely reflect social background characteristics. It testifies to the well-integrated character of the parliamentary party. Some minor associations have been found between, for example, non-public school background and greater receptiveness to social reform, but such associations are extremely fine. One explanation of this is the effects of 'social insulation' which a public school education can produce. Not dissimilarly, a study of free parliamentary voting on issues of conscience in the 1960s [22] (capital punishment, homosexuality, abortion, divorce, Sunday entertainment) suggested associations across the parties with, in this case, young, professional Members tending to be most susceptible to reforming positions, but in general the social homogeneity of the Conservative Party at Westminster contributes to its essential cohesiveness. What splits have occurred have been temporary alliances concerned with specific objectives and have been pacified by common social origins. Even the gulf which has appeared recently between the so-called Heath and Thatcher wings of the party is not really associated with any socio-economic cleavages. Cohesion, then, is one result of the narrow recruitment profile of the Conservative Party.

Labour: the cumulation of social and attitudinal cleavages

The impact of distinct socio-economic groupings in the Parliamentary Labour Party appears, in contrast to the Conservative Party, to have a divisive effect. Both in terms of association between background and political attitude, and as a symbolic factor in a party whose foundation was partly motivated by a desire to get more working men into Parliament, the embourgeoisement of the Labour Party has made unity within the parliamentary party that much more precarious. Unlike the Conservative Party, social and attitudinal cleavages have tended to reinforce each other. And change in the composition of the parliamentary party has, to some extent, been reflected in the changing composition of its electoral support in the country.

Before looking at social—attitudinal associations in the PLP, it is worth reasserting that such associations should not be taken to be causal relationships [23]. Because two variables are correlated, this cannot be taken to imply that one variable is the cause of the other. Certainly this cannot be demonstrated in the absence of any consideration of other possible factors, neither should the aggregate data be taken to task for not providing accounts or explanations of individual deviations from aggregate norms. Much of the foundations of social science are constructed upon our understandings of groups and classes rather than individuals, and where individuals do differ from the generality of groups, this must be taken to be one of the costs of an imperfect science which deals with humans rather than inanimate objects with consistent properties and tendencies. These qualifications aisde, strong associations have been found between social and attitudinal groupings within the PLP [24]. The general effect of social changes in the Labour Party over these three decades does coincide with distinct changes in policy preferences.

The most purposeful and systematic mapping of backbench opinion during this period is the work which has been performed on the analysis of Early Day Motions [25]. The associations between signatories and background characteristics tends to confirm that there are three, fairly distinct, groups within the PLP. Although these groups are only separable by emphasis or tendency, they are nevertheless recognisable. In very general terms, the established professions are most associated with a liberal stance within the party on, for example, humanitarian and Third World issues. They have also, in broad terms, tended to be the part-time parliamentarians in the party [26]. But the important differentiation occurs between the new professions (including journalists who have been placed in the miscellaneous group) and the workers who they are replacing. Traditionally, the workers have been strong on the material (bread and butter) issues and more moderate on ideological positions [27], whilst the new professions are much more strongly associated with the wider ideas and principles of socialism [28]. It is not surprising that these two groups should adopt divergent lines. The working class have most frequently become involved in political life in order to improve living standards. They have been much less concerned with any grand strategy and, coming up the hard way, have been more impressed by the realities and limitations of political change. The middle class, with their more liberal education and apparently greater visions, have concerned themselves with the wider opportunities for socialism. In the polarised terms so beloved by political journalists, this tends to put the workers on the Right of the party and the new professions on its Left. The changing configuration of Labour's parliamentary recruitment has consequently been accompanied by a greater concern with ideological issues in the PLP [29]. Even in the sponsored seats, the workers have now largely been replaced by middle class recruits, and the trade union MPs who have been elected since 1964 have moved noticeably to the Left of the party. Moreover in the last decade there has been a shift among the newly recruited workers to a more material leftism. The transformation of the Parliamentary Labour Party, therefore, does not simply reflect changing opportunities for working class involvement in parliamentary politics, but also coincides with changing political opinions. And the broad association between background and attitude compounds existing cleavages.

A further factor in the Labour Party is that symbolic representation has an importance which is not found in the other parties. One motivation behind the formation of the Labour Movement was to get more workers into Parliament. A motion set before the Founding Conference of the Labour Representation Committee on 27 February 1900 was to 'secure a better representation of the interests of labour in the House of Commons.' Some delegates even wanted to restrict Labour candidatures to working men and whilst Keir Hardie managed to persuade the conference to widen nomination to those sympathetic to the Labour Movement, this preference for 'actual representation' has remained in the minds of many supporters ever since. In the early part of this century in particular, the desire to achieve places for working men in the Commons was of more immediate concern than any programmatic goals [30]. Until 1945, workers formed the bulk of the parliamentary party, but since that date this section of the parliamentary group has been rapidly eroded. The search for more articulate and able parliamentarians, to compete with the other parties and widen its electoral support, has resulted in the severance of most of its direct representational links with the working class. In view of its origins, the increasing exclusion of workers in the PLP is of some importance.

There is a distinction between having sympathy with the working class and having actual working experience. It is possible to be *with* somebody without being *of* them, and for many traditional Labour supporters this is a vital distinction. This is especially true of some trade unionists [31]. The image which Labour presents is seen to be almost as fundamental as its policies and programmes: a shared identity is as important as empathy or common doctrine. And, of course, although the Labour Party remains a party of the working class, it can no longer claim that its parliamentary party is a domain for worker representatives. It is a favourite pastime of the media to publicise the comfortable lifestyles which many Labour leaders now enjoy. This increasing social distance between Labour supporters and parliamentarians could serve to alienate the working class from traditional party politics. The miners are now one of the few groups who ensure the return of workers to Westminster. Their leader, Dennis Skinner, has pointed out the importance of continuing this practice:

> Is it important to have people in Parliament who know about mining from practical experience and do not have to 'swot up' about pneumoconiosis medical panels in order to comment on the subject . . . Perhaps some would say on the basis of enthusiasm and activity they (non-miners) are worthy aspirants. But could they accurately reflect the views of those born and bred in the harsh pit environment? [32]

Clearly, this MP believes they could not, and there is good reason to believe that he is not alone in holding this opinion.

At the same time that the embourgeoisement of the parliamentary party occurs, this transformation percolates throughout the party structure. At the highest level of the party structure, the National Executive Committee has undergone the same changes in social composition [33]. At a lower level in the structure there has, of course, been considerable concern over the decrease in working class involvement in constituency and ward party politics [34]. And it is, incidentally, the demise of some urban constituency parties which is held to be largely responsible for their infiltration by radical elements within the party. Certainly the party stalwarts of twenty, or even ten years ago, are much less conspicuous now. Abstention by the working class is argued to be one consequence of a distanced party leadership. Even at the level of electoral support, the class/party connection has weakened. In 1964, 83 per cent of Labour's votes came from the working class. Ten years later, and despite the fact that the February 1974 election was fought on pronounced class issues, the proportion of Labour's working class electoral support had fallen to 73 per cent [35]. This is still fairly solid support, but this linear trend portends significant changes in electoral behaviour.

In its early years the Labour Party was overwhelmingly committed to improving the conditions of life for the working man. But as it has assumed the mantle of a governing party, as it has since 1945, its programmes have become less sectoral. In terms of its parliamentary composition, its party structure and, to a lesser degree, its electoral support, the relationship with the working class is weakening. Labour now projects itself as a party fit to govern rather than as a party of the workers. It still attracts the majority of working class votes, but this attachment is less committed [36]. The social transformation of the Parliamentary Labour Party since 1945 reflects not only declining opportunities for working class involvement in parliamentary politics, but also corresponds with the new directions and national status assumed by the Labour Party since that time.

The professionalisation of politics

Any study of post-war recruitment to the British House of Commons would be incomplete without some reference to the professionalisation of politics which has occurred over this period and especially over the last decade in response to the new professional recruits. Much has been written in recent years about how the middle class recruits of the sixties, especially on the Labour benches, have made a considerable impact on Parliament [37]. This need not, consequently, be chronicled in detail here, except to say that the common theme running throughout these accounts is how the new professional men, not content to be mere party 'lobby fodder', have sought considerably extended opportunities for backbench influence and scrutiny. The repeated demands for parliamentary reform owe much to these more active and enthusiastic parliamentarians, as indeed does much of the progress which has been achieved in this field since 1966. An extended system of select committees, better library and research facilities, better accommodation and secretarial assistance and funds for research projects by opposition parties are some of the developments which immediately spring to mind. For above all, politics has, in this period, established itself as a profession in its own right. This is not to deny that Members still have axes to grind, interests or partial views of the needs of the nation, but in the vast majority of cases a place in Parliament is sought after for reasons other than personal gain. The Members which Namier spoke of – the predestined Parliament man, the 'country party', the social climbers and those seeking promotion in their extra-parliamentary careers – are relatively rare in the House today [38]. Politics has become much more of a full-time profession and, indeed, this very fact has caused some of the less committed MPs to return to their former careers where the financial rewards were often far greater. Of course, some have resisted this movement towards full-time politics, but the process is almost inevitable. Philip Buck's whole thesis is directed towards a consideration of the professional in politics, and he observes that: 'In the days of urban, industrial societies it is inevitable that in all democratic governments a large proportion of the leaders should become professionals . . . The tasks of present-day government demand professional skills and experience' [39]. There is good reason for believing that the last five elections have resulted in the return of more skilled and, given their more youthful entry, more potentially experienced MPs. 'The full-time professional MP cannot be regretted', writes Bernard Crick, 'he is a natural response to the volume and complexities of modern legislation' [40]. If the main cost of changing political recruitment in the post-war period has been the exclusion of workers from the Commons, it seems appropriate to record that the main benefit has been the election of more professionally conscious parliamentarians.

Achieving wider representation

Prediction is a hazardous and speculative task, but it seems appropriate, by way of a postscript, to conclude with a few rather tentative thoughts on the future for parliamentary recruitment.

On the basis of past evidence we may expect the dominant trends of the last three decades to continue. Certainly there is no sign of any revival of worker representatives in the Labour Party. It is a paradox that as Labour increasingly opens its ranks to meritocratic competition, the more exclusive the social composition of the parliamentary party becomes. Few new workers are coming forward and even in the trade union seats, outside possibly the ranks of a couple of staunch labour unions, departing worker MPs are being replaced by new middle class political careerists. The process is time-lagged by the current worker Members holding safe seats, but there is every reason to contemplate the continuing embourgeoisement of the Parliamentary Labour Party. On the Conservative side, processes of change are much less pronounced and more gradual. This party's losses have occurred in the upper strata of society, and there is no suggestion of any weakening of the business routes to Westminster or, indeed, of any change in the fundamentally homogeneous character of this parliamentary party. The consequence is a narrowing, though still distinct between parties, recruitment base. The Nationalist parties have not disturbed this process by the introduction of any novel social breeds [41].

There are three possible changes which could operate to widen the pool from which Members of Parliament are selected. One might be ascribed to party changes and the others to constitutional reforms.

Undoubtedly one of the dominant characteristics of party politics during the last thirty years has been declining party memberships and this is common to both major parties. In the case of the Labour Party, activism has been frequently associated with the working class. The reduction of individual, as opposed to corporate, memberships is therefore largely explained by workers' abstentions. One important way of widening the opportunities for working class involvement in parliamentary politics is consequently in the hands of the Labour Party itself through the revival of a healthy Party structure in the country. In their concern for stressing 'ability', the post-war Labour Party has tended to neglect many of its foundations in the constituencies. This partly explains the current concern within the party for the way in which small, and unrepresentative, caucuses can assume power in decaying local parties. Specific recommendations about widening selection procedures are now fairly commonplace [42].

A second, and constitutional change, which might affect the nature of political recruitment is the introduction of a proportional representation electoral system which is based upon multi-member constituencies. The hopes of the electoral reformers in Britain have received a boost in recent years with increasing scepticism about the desirability of maintaining a two-party system [43] and also speculation about the introduction of PR systems for the European elections and the proposed Scottish and Welsh assemblies [44]. And though the evidence is slight, there is some reason to believe that a by-product of electoral reform might be a wider variety of candidates. This can be illustrated by the case of women. In multi-member constituencies, a party which is 'reluctant to select a woman as its *only* candidate may be much more willing to include her as one of a list of several men' [45]. The same reasoning can be applied to other presently under-represented groups. From the party's viewpoint such a practice might even have the effect of widening its electoral appeal. The effect upon minor social groups can also operate at election as well as nomination stage, since there is opportunity for voters to express preferences between candidates of the same party.

A third, and probably more distant, possibility is the opportunity afforded by some transfer from territorial to functional representation. The most common suggestions on these lines involve the recurring ideas about reforming the House of Lords and the concept of an Industrial Parliament. Churchill in his 1930 Romanes Lecture argued that the Westminster Parliament was less competent to deal with the economic issues which were coming to dominate politics [46]. And though nothing happened, the idea of formalising industry—trade union—government relations has been floated at intervals ever since. It came one step closer in the early sixties with the establishment of the National Economic Development Council and the operation of a 'social contract' since 1974 between the Labour Government and the unions is a further movement in this direction. The extent to which such a body would, in fact, bring new groups into the formal decision-making arena would naturally depend upon the methods of selection/election employed by the interests involved.

This speculation aside, this short study of post-war legislative recruitment in Britain suggest that the predominant trends of the past ten elections show every sign of continuing. The Conservative Party remains a largely exclusive and homogeneous body. The Labour Party has undergone considerable change. It remains diverse in its composition, but one important group, the workers, are rapidly being displaced from the Westminster benches. The Labour Party continues the representation *of* labour but no longer *by* labour. All of this means a Parliament which has become increasingly professional in its background and aspirations yet uncharacteristic of, and some would argue isolated from, the electorate whom it represents.

Notes

[1]   B.R. Crick, *The Reform of Parliament*, 2nd Edition, Weidenfeld, London, 1968, p. 55.

[2]   *Committee on the Management of Local Government*, Volume 2, 'The Local Government Councillor', HMSO, 1968.

[3]   I. Crewe (ed.), *British Political Sociology Yearbook*, p. 101.

[4]   Nesta Wyn Ellis, *Dear Elector*, Coronet, London, 1974, p. 45. For a fuller discussion see R.W. Johnson, 'The British Political Elite 1955—1972', *European Journal of Sociology*, 1973, pp. 68—77.

[5]   A.H. Birch, *Representation*, Macmillan, London, 1971, p. 54.

[6]   W. Bagehot, *The English Constitution*, Fontana, London, 1963, p. 150.

[7]   J.P. Mackintosh, 'The Declining Respect for the Law', in A. King (ed.), *Why is Britain Becoming Harder to Govern?*, BBC Publications, London, 1976.

[8]   M. Currell, *Political Woman*, Croom Helm, London, 1974, p. 35.

[9] See *Small Firms: Report of the Committee of Inquiry on Small Firms*, Cmnd. 4811, HMSO (The Bolton Report) 1971.

[10] See Bolton Committee Research Report No. 7: 'Attitude and Motivation'.

[11] The present Minister is R. Cryer. The inquiry, under Harold Lever, was announced in September 1977.

[12] See P. Self and H. Storing, *The State and the Farmer*, Allen and Unwin, London, 1962, and S.J. Rogers, *New Society*, 5 February 1970. An illustration of this influence also appears in Harold Macmillan's memoirs for the early months of 1957.

[13] See especially, B. Hindess, *The Decline of Working Class Politics*, MacGibbon and Kee, London, 1971 and T. Forester, *The Labour Party and the Working Class*, Heinemann, London, 1976.

[14] See I. Crewe, Bo. Sarlvik, J. Alt, 'Partisan Dealignment in Britain 1964–74', *British Journal of Political Science*, April 1977.

[15] See A. King, op. cit., R. Rose, 'Overloaded Government; The Problem Outlined', *I.P.S.A. Congress*, Edinburgh 1976; J. Douglas, 'The Overloaded Crown', *British Journal of Political Science*, 1976.

[16] See proposals of the *Bullock Committee on Industrial Democracy*, 1977.

[17] P. Seyd, 'Factionalism within the Conservative Party', *Government and Opposition*, 1972.

[18] See Finer, Berrington and Bartholomew, op. cit., pp. 104–14 and Berrington, op. cit., p. 183–4.

[19] Crewe (et al.), op. cit., p. 169.

[20] Ibid., p. 151.

[21] Finer (et al.), op. cit., pp. 104–21; Berrington, op. cit., pp. 165–84.

[22] P.G. Richards, *Parliament and Conscience*, Allen and Unwin, London, 1970, Chapter 9.

[23] A convincing defence of the social background approach to understanding parliamentary opinion is given in Berrington, op. cit., Chapter 1.

[24] I lean heavily here upon the findings of Finer (et al.), op. cit., Berrington, op. cit., and Berrington and Leece, op. cit.

[25] Ibid.

[26] Finer (et al.), p. 63.

[27] Ibid., pp. 45 and 60; Berrington, p. 200.

[28] Finer (et al.), p. 64; Berrington, p. 200.

[29] Berrington and Leece, op. cit., pp. 36–8.

[30] R. Rose, 'Class and Party Divisions: Britain as a Test-Case', *Sociology* 2, pp. 129–62.

[31] See Richard Crossman's interview with Jack Jones reproduced in *The Listener*, 4 April 1974.

[32] Dennis Skinner MP, *The Miner*, September–October 1976.

[33] V.J. Hanby, 'A Changing Labour Elite: The National Executive Committee of the Labour Party', in Crewe (ed.), op. cit., pp. 126–58.

[34] Hindess, op. cit.

[35] Crewe (et al.), op. cit., p. 169.

[36] Ibid., p. 151.

[37] See, for example, P.G. Richards, *The Backbenchers*, Faber, London, 1972; R. Butt, *The Power of Parliament*, Constable, London, 1969; A.H. Hanson and B.R. Crick (eds), *The Commons in Transition*, Fontana, London, 1970; A. Barker and M. Rush, *The Member of Parliament and His Information*, Allen and Unwin, London, 1970; J.P. Mackintosh, 'Specialist Committees in the House of Commons: Have They Failed?', *Waverley Paper*, University of Edinburgh; S.A. Walkland and M. Ryle (eds), *The Commons in the Seventies*, Fontana, London, 1977.

[38] Namier, op. cit.

[39] Buck, op. cit., pp. 87–8.

[40] Crick, op. cit., p. 56.

[41] Despite Rush's observations in Walkland and Ryle, op. cit., p. 36.

[42] Paterson, op. cit.

[43] See S.E. Finer (ed.), *Adversary Politics and Electoral Reform*, Anthony Wigram, London, 1975.

[44] The general preference for a PR system for any new Scottish and Welsh assemblies was one of the few common themes in the *Report of the Royal Commission on the Constitution*, Cmnd. 5460, 1973. In the event the electoral reformers lost both battles: PR was rejected for the devolved assemblies and the European elections.

[45] E. Lakeman, op. cit., p. 31.

[46] W.S. Churchill, *Parliamentary Government and the Economic Problem*, Oxford University Press, London, 1930. See more generally, J. Douglas, op. cit., for a review of the proposals.

Appendix

This appendix contains demographic data on *departing* MPs. For reasons of space these were not included in the main body of the book, but by comparing these tables with their equivalents for *new* MPs they sharpen the changing configurations of recruitment patterns which cohort analysis produces.

Table 9.1

Departing Members contesting seats before first election

Election	Conservative Total MPs	Con- tests	No. MPs	%	Labour Total MPs	Con- tests	No. MPs	%	Other Total MPs	Con- tests	No. MPs
1945	45	1	6	13·3	132	1	16	12·1	21	1	1
		2	1	2·2		2	7	5·3		2	1
		3	–	–		3	5	3·8		3	1
		4	–	–		4	3	2·3		4	1
		5	–	–		5	–	–		5	–
		Nil	38	84·5		Nil	101	76·5		Nil	17
		Total	45	100·0		Total	132	100·0		Total	21
1950	24	1	2	8·3	37	1	2	5·4	4	1	–
		2	–	–		2	4	10·8		2	–
		3	–	–		3	–	–		3	–
		4	–	–		4	–	–		4	–
		5	–	–		5	–	–		5	–
		Nil	22	91·7		Nil	31	83·8		Nil	4
		Total	24	100·0		Total	37	100·0		Total	4
1951	56	1	11	19·7	49	1	7	14·3	2	1	–
		2	1	1·8		2	2	4·1		2	–
		3	–	–		3	1	2·0		3	–
		4	–	–		4	1	2·0		4	–
		5	–	–		5	1	2·0		5	–
		Nil	44	78·5		Nil	37	75·6		Nil	2
		Total	56	100·0		Total	49	100·0		Total	2
1955	83	1	18	21·7	62	1	7	11·3	4	1	–
		2	4	4·8		2	3	4·8		2	1
		3	–	–		3	3	4·8		3	–
		4	–	–		4	–	–		4	–
		5	–	–		5	–	–		5	–
		Nil	61	73·5		Nil	49	79·1		Nil	3
		Total	83	100·0		Total	62	100·0		Total	4
1959	115	1	26	22·6	56	1	4	7·1	4	1	1
		2	14	12·2		2	7	12·5		2	–
		3	3	2·6		3	1	1·8		3	–
		4	1	0·9		4	–	–		4	–
		5	–	–		5	–	–		5	–
		Nil	71	61·7		Nil	44	78·6		Nil	3
		Total	115	100·0		Total	56	100·0		Total	4
1964	54	1	19	35·2	25	1	6	24·0	2	1	1
		2	5	9·3		2	2	8·0		2	–
		3	1	1·9		3	–	–		3	–
		4	–	–		4	1	4·0		4	–
		5	–	–		5	1	4·0		5	–
		Nil	29	53·6		Nil	15	60·0		Nil	1
		Total	54	100·0		Total	25	100·0		Total	2

(Table continued on facing page)

Table 9.1 (continued)

Election	Total MPs	Conservative Con-tests	No. MPs	%	Total MPs	Labour Con-tests	No. MPs	%	Total MPs	Other Con-tests	No. MPs
1966	42	1	9	21·4	117	1	31	26·5	4	1	1
		2	5	11·9		2	15	12·8		2	–
		3	1	2·3		3	5	4·3		3	1
		4	1	2·3		4	–	–		4	–
		5	–	–		5	–	–		5	–
		Nil	26	62·1		Nil	66	56·4		Nil	2
		Total	42	100·0		Total	117	100·0		Total	4
1970	88	1	17	19.3	49	1	13	26.5	2	1	–
		2	18	20.4		2	5	10.2		2	–
		3	3	3.4		3	3	6.1		3	–
		4	–	–		4	–	–		4	–
		5	–	–		5	–	–		5	–
		Nil	50	56.8		Nil	28	57.2		Nil	2
		Total	88	100·0		Total	49	100·0		Total	2
Feb. 1974	33	1	7	21.2	11	1	2	18.2	5	1	2
		2	5	15.2		2	2	18.2		2	1
		3	1	3.0		3	–	–		3	–
		4	–	–		4	–	–		4	–
		5	–	–		5	–	–		5	–
		Nil	20	60.6		Nil	7	63.6		Nil	2
		Total	33	100·0		Total	11	100·0		Total	5

Table 9.2
Age distribution of departing Members

(a) Conservative

Age	1945 No. MPs	%	1950 No. MPs	%	1951 No. MPs	%	1955 No. MPs	%	1959 No. MPs	%	1964 No. MPs	%
21–29	–	–	–	–	–	–	–	–	2	1·7	–	–
30–39	5	12·2	4	16·7	5	9·8	7	8·5	9	7·8	5	9·3
40–49	6	14·6	6	25·0	9	17·7	15	18·3	34	29·6	8	14·8
50–59	12	29·3	5	20·8	23	45·0	32	39·1	47	40·9	20	37·0
60–69	11	26·8	5	20·8	8	15·7	23	28·0	20	17·4	18	33·3
70+	7	17·1	4	16·7	6	11·8	5	6·1	3	2·6	3	5·6
Total	41	100·0	24	100·0	51	100·0	82	100·0	115	100·0	54	100·0
INA	4		0		5		1		0		0	

Age	1966 No. MPs	%	1970 No. MPs	%	Feb. 1974 No. MPs	%
21–29	–	–	–	–	1	3·1
30–39	2	4·8	7	8·0	2	6·2
40–49	4	9·5	12	13·8	8	25·0
50–59	16	38·1	26	29·9	13	40·6
60–69	20	47·6	30	34·5	6	18·9
70+	–	–	12	13·8	2	6·2
Total	42	100·0	87	100·0	31	100·0
INA	0		1		1	

(b) Labour

Age	1945 No. MPs	%	1950 No. MPs	%	1951 No. MPs	%	1955 No. MPs	%	1959 No. MPs	%	1964 No. MPs	%
21–29	1	0·9	–	–	–	–	–	–	–	–	–	–
30–39	9	8·3	3	8·3	4	8·3	1	1·7	1	1·8	1	4·2
40–49	27	25·0	10	27·7	10	20·9	8	13·4	3	5·4	–	–
50–59	29	26·9	11	30·6	8	16·6	20	33·3	15	26·8	2	8·3
60–69	29	26·9	6	16·7	21	43·8	20	33·3	22	39·2	17	70·9
70+	13	12·0	6	16·7	5	10·4	11	18·3	15	26·8	4	16·6
Total	108	100·0	36	100·0	48	100·0	60	100·0	56	100·0	24	100·0
INA	24		1		1		2		0		1	

(Table continued on facing page)

Table 9.2 (continued)

Age	1966 No. MPs	1966 %	1970 No. MPs	1970 %	Feb.1974 No. MPs	Feb.1974 %
21–29	5	4·3	1	2·0	–	–
30–39	26	22·2	2	4·1	1	9·1
40–49	10	8·5	9	18·4	3	27·3
50–59	22	18·8	4	8·2	1	9·1
60–69	39	33·3	21	42·8	5	45·4
70+	15	12·9	12	24·5	1	9·1
Total	117	100·0	49	100·0	11	100·0
INA	0		0		0	

(c) Others

Age	1945	1950	1951	1955	1959	1964	1966	1970	Feb. 1974
21–29	–	–	–	2	–	–	–	1	–
30–39	1	–	–	1	–	–	3	1	1
40–49	7	2	1	–	2	1	–	–	1
50–59	3	1	–	–	1	1	–	–	3
60–69	6	1	–	1	–	–	1	–	–
70+	1	–	1	–	1	–	–	–	–
Total	18	4	2	4	4	2	4	2	5
INA	3	0	·0	0	0	0	0	0	0

Table 9.3
Education of departing MPs, by election

| | 1945 | | | 1950 | | | 1951 | | |
	Con	Lab	Oth	Con	Lab	Oth	Con	Lab	Oth
Elementary only	–	45	1	–	12	–	1	13	–
Elementary +	–	10	1	–	1	–	–	7	–
Secondary only	2	15	2	1	2	–	1	4	2
Secondary +	–	2	–	–	–	–	–	2	–
Secondary/professional	1	9	2	–	8	1	–	1	–
Secondary/university	7	22	5	2	8	1	5	14	–
Secondary/service college	–	–	–	–	–	1	–	–	–
Secondary/service/univ.	–	–	–	–	–	–	–	–	–
Private only	–	–	–	–	–	–	1	–	–
Private/service college	–	–	–	–	–	–	–	–	–
Private/university	–	–	–	–	–	–	1	–	–
Private/service/university	–	–	–	–	–	–	–	–	–
Private/professional	–	1	–	1	–	–	–	–	–
Public only	6	3	2	2	–	–	9	1	–
Public/professional	1	2	1	–	–	–	1	–	–
Public/service college	3	2	–	6	–	–	7	–	–
Public/'Oxbridge'	16	8	6	11	1	–	22	5	–
Public/other university	2	4	–	1	3	–	4	1	–
Foreign/UK university	–	–	–	–	–	–	–	–	–
Abroad	–	–	–	–	–	–	–	–	–
INA	7	9	1	–	2	1	4	1	–
Total	45	132	21	24	37	4	56	49	2
All public schools	28	19	9	20	4	–	43	7	–
Eton	7	2	–	11	–	–	14	–	–
Oxford	6	11	6	7	1	–	17	4	–
Cambridge	11	5	1	5	1	–	8	1	–
London	–	10	1	–	3	–	2	2	–
Wales	1	2	–	–	2	1	–	2	–
Scotland	5	4	2	–	1	–	–	4	–
Ireland	2	–	–	1	1	–	–	1	–
Foreign	–	–	–	–	1	–	2	2	–
Other universities	–	2	1	1	2	–	3	4	–
All universities	25	34	11	14	12	1	32	20	0

| | 1955 | | | 1959 | | | 1964 | | |
	Con	Lab	Oth	Con	Lab	Oth	Con	Lab	Oth
Elementary only	–	19	1	1	16	–	–	6	–
Elementary +	–	14	–	1	12	–	1	4	–
Secondary only	2	6	–	8	6	–	5	4	–
Secondary +	–	1	–	–	1	–	–	1	–
Secondary/professional	1	3	–	4	2	–	1	2	–
Secondary/university	3	7	2	10	9	1	3	3	2
Secondary/service coll.	–	–	–	–	–	–	–	–	–
Secondary/service/univ.	–	–	–	1	–	–	–	–	–
Private only	3	–	–	1	1	–	1	–	–
Private/service college	–	–	–	3	–	–	4	–	–

(Table continued on facing page)

Table 9.3 (continued)

	1955 Con	Lab	Oth	1959 Con	Lab	Oth	1964 Con	Lab	Oth
Private/university	–	–	–	–	–	–	–	–	–
Private/service/univ.	–	–	–	–	–	–	–	–	–
Private/professional	–	–	–	–	–	–	–	–	–
Public only	10	1	–	17	3	1	3	–	–
Public/professional	2	–	–	8	–	–	1	–	–
Public/service college	6	–	–	7	–	–	8	–	–
Public/'Oxbridge'	45	7	–	47	5	1	22	2	–
Public/other university	7	3	–	6	–	1	3	3	–
Foreign/UK university	–	–	–	–	–	–	–	–	–
Abroad	–	–	–	–	–	–	–	–	–
INA	4	1	1	1	1	–	2	–	–
Total	83	62	4	115	56	4	54	25	2
All public schools	70	11	–	85	8	3	37	5	–
Eton	21	1	–	20	2	–	10	–	–
Oxford	29	3	–	29	6	–	12	2	–
Cambridge	16	4	–	22	1	2	11	1	–
London	1	5	–	4	2	–	1	3	–
Wales	–	1	2	–	1	–	–	1	1
Scotland	4	2	–	3	2	–	1	–	1
Ireland	1	–	–	2	–	–	–	–	–
Foreign	1	–	–	2	–	–	1	–	–
Other universities	3	2	–	2	2	1	2	1	–
All universities	55	17	2	64	14	3	28	8	2

	1966 Con	Lab	Oth	1970 Con	Lab	Oth	Feb. 1974 Con	Lab	Oth
Elementary only	–	25	–	1	4	–	–	2	–
Elementary +	–	11	–	–	10	–	–	3	–
Secondary only	1	15	1	2	9	–	4	–	–
Secondary +	–	3	–	–	–	–	–	–	–
Secondary/professional	–	6	–	5	1	1	–	–	–
Secondary/university	3	24	–	4	13	1	3	3	–
Secondary/service coll.	–	–	–	–	–	–	–	–	–
Secondary/service/univ.	–	–	–	–	–	–	–	–	–
Private only	–	1	1	1	–	–	–	–	–
Private/service college	2	1	–	–	–	–	–	–	–
Private/university	–	–	–	–	–	–	–	–	–
Private/service/univ.	–	–	1	2	–	–	–	–	–
Private/professional	–	–	–	–	–	–	–	–	–
Public only	5	6	–	16	1	–	5	1	2
Public/professional	4	2	–	4	–	–	1	–	–
Public/service college	1	–	–	6	–	–	2	–	–
Public/'Oxbridge'	24	12	1	36	9	–	18	1	2
Public/other university	1	10	–	9	2	–	–	–	1
Foreign/UK university	–	–	–	–	–	–	–	–	–
Abroad	–	–	–	1	–	–	–	–	–
INA	1	1	–	1	–	–	–	–	–
Total	42	117	4	88	49	2	33	11	5

(Table continued overleaf)

Table 9.3 (continued)

	1966			1970			Feb. 1974		
	Con	Lab	Oth	Con	Lab	Oth	Con	Lab	Oth
All public schools	25	30	1	71	12	–	26	2	5
Eton	10	1	–	17	1	–	7	–	–
Oxford	17	9	2	20	8	–	15	1	1
Cambridge	8	8	–	19	1	–	4	1	–
London	–	10	–	4	7	–	–	–	–
Wales	–	1	–	–	2	–	–	2	–
Scotland	1	7	–	–	3	–	–	–	–
Ireland	1	1	–	2	–	1	1	–	–
Foreign	–	2	–	–	–	–	–	–	–
Other universities	1	8	–	6	3	–	1	1	2
All universities	28	46	2	1	24	1	21	5	3

Table 9.4

Some major educational backgrounds of departing MPs

(a) Conservative

	1945	1950	1951	1955	1959	1964	1966	1970	Feb. 1974
Elementary*	–	–	1·9	–	1·7	1·9	–	1·1	–
Public/Oxbridge	42·1	45·8	42·4	56·9	41·2	38·5	58·5	41·4	54·5
Eton	18·4	45·8	26·9	26·6	17·5	19·2	24·4	19·5	21·2
Public school	74·0	83·4	82·7	88·6	74·6	71·2	61·0	81·6	78·8
'Oxbridge'	44·7	50·0	48·1	56·9	44·7	44·3	61·0	44·8	57·6
All universities	65·8	58·3	61·6	69·6	56·2	53·9	68·3	58·6	63·6

(b) Labour

	1945	1950	1951	1955	1959	1964	1966	1970	Feb. 1974
Elementary*	44·7	37·2	41·7	54·1	50·9	40·0	27·0	28·6	45·4
Secondary/university	17·9	22·8	29·2	11·5	16·4	12·0	27·0	26·5	36·4
Public/Oxbridge	6·5	2·9	10·4	11·5	9·1	8·0	10·2	18·4	9·1
Public school	15·5	11·4	14·6	18·0	14·5	20·0	25·6	24·5	18·2
Oxbridge	13·0	5·7	10·4	11·5	12·7	12·0	16·1	18·4	18·2
London	8·1	8·6	4·2	8·2	3·6	12·0	10·2	14·3	–
All universities	27·7	34·3	41·7	27·9	25·5	32·0	46·7	49·0	45·4

* Includes 'elementary plus'

Table 9.5
Occupations of departing MPs, by election

	1945			1950			1951		
	Con	Lab	Oth	Con	Lab	Oth	Con	Lab	Oth
Barrister	5	6	1	4	5	–	12	3	–
Solicitor	1	4	–	1	3	1	1	1	–
Ch. surveyor/engineer	1	4	2	–	2	–	2	1	–
Civil service/local govt.	1	2	–	1	1	–	1	1	–
Services	5	2	–	5	–	–	4	–	–
Diplomatic services	–	–	1	1	–	–	2	–	–
Lecturer	1	3	3	–	1	–	2	6	–
School teacher	1	8	–	–	4	–	–	4	–
Doctor/dentist	1	4	2	–	–	–	–	2	–
Ch. accountant/secretary	–	2	–	–	–	–	2	–	–
Scientific worker	–	1	–	–	–	–	–	–	–
Minister of religion	1	1	–	1	2	–	–	–	–
Social worker	–	–	–	–	–	–	–	–	–
Total (professions)	17	37	9	13	18	1	26	18	0
Small business	–	–	–	–	–	–	–	1	–
Director	17	4	1	4	1	1	15	–	–
Banker/financier	–	1	–	2	–	–	1	–	–
Executive/management	–	4	–	–	1	–	–	3	–
Commerce/insurance	2	–	–	1	–	–	2	1	–
Business consultant	–	–	1	–	1	–	–	1	–
Clerical	–	2	–	–	–	–	–	–	–
Total (business)	19	11	2	7	3	1	18	6	0
White collar	–	5	–	–	1	–	–	–	1
Political worker	–	–	1	–	–	–	–	2	–
Trade union official	–	20	–	–	4	–	–	7	–
Farmer/landowner	6	2	3	2	–	1	9	–	1
Housewife	–	1	–	–	1	–	–	–	–
Student	–	–	–	1	–	–	–	–	–
Journalist/author	1	12	5	1	–	1	3	5	–
Public relations	–	1	–	–	–	–	–	–	–
Actor	–	–	–	–	–	–	–	–	–
Pilot	–	–	–	–	–	–	–	–	–
Policeman	–	1	–	–	–	–	–	–	–
Total (miscellaneous)	7	42	9	4	6	2	12	14	2
Railwayman	–	9	–	–	1	–	–	3	–
Miner	–	11	–	–	3	–	–	4	–
Skilled worker	–	8	1	–	3	–	–	3	–
Semi/unskilled worker	–	6	–	–	3	–	–	1	–
Total (workers)	0	34	1	0	10	0	0	11	0
INA	2	8	0	0	0	0	0	0	0
Grand total	45	132	21	24	37	4	56	49	2

(Table continued overleaf)

Table 9.5 (continued)

	1955 Con	1955 Lab	1955 Oth	1959 Con	1959 Lab	1959 Oth	1964 Con	1964 Lab	1964 Oth
Barrister	12	4	2	17	5	1	6	2	1
Solicitor	3	2	–	2	–	1	2	1	–
Ch. surveyor/engineer	1	–	–	4	2	–	1	–	–
Civil service/local govt.	–	–	–	1	–	–	–	1	–
Services	9	–	–	12	–	–	9	–	–
Diplomatic services	3	–	–	3	1	–	3	–	–
Lecturer	–	2	–	–	4	–	2	1	–
School teacher	–	4	–	–	2	–	1	3	–
Doctor/dentist	1	2	–	2	2	–	1	1	–
Ch.accountant/secretary	1	–	–	5	–	–	–	–	–
Scientific worker	1	–	–	–	1	–	–	–	–
Minister of religion	–	–	–	–	–	–	–	2	–
Social worker	2	–	–	–	–	–	1	–	–
Total (professions)	33	14	2	46	17	2	26	11	1
Small business	–	1	–	–	–	–	–	–	–
Director	22	4	–	43	2	–	14	1	–
Banker/financier	–	–	–	1	–	–	–	–	–
Executive/management	4	1	–	1	–	–	1	1	–
Commerce/insurance	3	–	–	7	–	1	4	–	–
Business consultant	–	–	–	2	–	–	1	–	–
Clerical	–	–	–	–	1	–	–	–	–
Total (business)	29	6	0	54	3	1	20	2	0
White collar	1	2	1	–	3	–	–	2	–
Political worker	2	–	–	–	1	–	1	–	–
Trade union official	–	5	–	–	12	–	–	2	–
Farmer/landowner	11	–	–	12	–	1	4	–	1
Housewife	1	–	–	1	–	–	–	–	–
Student	3	–	–	–	–	–	–	–	–
Journalist/author	1	5	–	1	3	–	1	–	–
Public relations	–	–	–	–	–	–	1	1	–
Actor	–	–	–	–	–	–	–	–	–
Pilot	–	–	–	–	–	–	–	–	–
Policeman	–	–	–	–	–	–	–	–	–
Total (miscellaneous)	19	12	1	14	19	1	7	5	1
Railwayman	–	9	–	–	3	–	–	2	–
Miner	–	9	–	–	7	–	–	3	–
Skilled worker	–	6	–	–	3	–	–	2	–
Semi/unskilled worker	–	3	1	–	3	–	–	–	–
Total (workers)	0	27	1	0	16	0	0	7	0
INA	2	3	0	1	1	0	1	0	0
Grand total	83	62	4	115	56	4	54	25	2

(Table continued on facing page)

Table 9.5 (continued)

	1966			1970			Feb. 1974		
	Con	Lab	Oth	Con	Lab	Oth	Con	Lab	Oth
Barrister	13	4	–	11	7	–	5	1	1
Solicitor	1	8	–	3	3	–	2	–	–
Ch.surveyor/engineer	1	4	–	1	1	–	–	–	–
Civil service/local govt.	–	2	–	–	1	–	–	–	–
Services	2	1	–	8	–	–	1	–	–
Diplomatic services	2	1	–	3	–	–	3	–	–
Lecturer	–	13	–	–	7	–	–	2	–
School teacher	–	6	–	2	3	1	–	–	–
Doctor/dentist	–	2	–	3	–	–	–	–	1
Ch.accountant/secretary	–	1	–	4	1	–	–	–	1
Scientific worker	–	–	–	–	–	–	–	1	–
Minister of religion	–	–	–	–	–	–	–	–	–
Social worker	–	–	–	1	–	–	–	–	–
Total (professions)	19	42	0	36	23	1	11	4	3
Small business	–	1	–	1	1	–	1	–	–
Director	18	6	1	23	–	–	6	–	–
Banker/financier	–	–	–	1	–	–	1	–	–
Executive/management	–	6	–	3	–	–	1	–	–
Commerce/insurance	1	1	–	2	–	–	2	–	–
Business consultant	–	1	1	–	1	–	1	–	–
Clerical	–	1	–	1	–	–	–	–	–
Total (business)	19	16	2	31	2	0	12	0	0
White collar	–	4	–	1	2	–	–	–	–
Political worker	–	1	–	1	1	–	–	–	–
Trade union official	–	10	–	–	5	–	–	2	1
Farmer/landowner	2	2	2	9	1	–	6	1	1
Housewife	–	2	–	–	1	–	1	–	–
Student	–	–	–	1	–	1	–	–	–
Journalist/author	2	14	–	5	3	–	3	1	–
Public relations	–	3	–	2	1	–	–	1	–
Actor	–	–	–	–	–	–	–	–	–
Pilot	–	–	–	–	–	–	–	–	–
Policeman	–	–	–	–	–	–	–	–	–
Total (miscellaneous)	4	36	2	19	14	1	10	5	2
Railwayman	–	4	–	–	1	–	–	–	–
Miner	–	9	–	–	5	–	–	–	–
Skilled worker	–	5	–	–	3	–	–	–	–
Semi/unskilled worker	–	5	–	–	1	–	–	2	–
Total (workers)	0	23	0	0	10	0	0	2	0
INA	0	0	0	2	0	0	0	0	0
Grand total	42	117	4	88	49	2	33	11	5

Table 9.6
Occupational backgrounds of departing Members (percentages)

(a) Conservative

	1945	1950	1951	1955	1959	1964	1966	1970	Feb. 1974
Professional	39·6	54·2	46·4	40·8	40·4	49·1	45·3	41·9	33·3
Business	44·2	29·1	32·2	35·8	47·4	37·8	45·3	36·0	36·4
Miscellaneous	16·2	16·7	21·4	23·4	12·2	13·1	9·4	22·1	30·3
Workers	–	–	–	–	–	–	–	–	–
	100·0	100·0	100·0	100·0	100·0	100·0	100·0	100·0	100·0
	n=45	n=24	n=56	n=83	n=115	n=54	n=42	n=88	n=33

(b) Labour

	1945	1950	1951	1955	1959	1964	1966	1970	Feb. 1974
Professional	29·8	48·7	36·8	23·7	30·9	44·0	35·9	46·9	36·4
Business	8·9	8·1	12·2	10·2	5·5	8·0	13·7	4·1	–
Miscellaneous	33·9	16·2	28·6	20·3	34·6	20·0	30·8	28·6	45·4
Workers	27·4	27·0	22·4	45·8	29·0	28·0	19·6	20·4	18·2
	100·0	100·0	100·0	100·0	100·0	100·0	100·0	100·0	100·0
	n=132	n=37	n=49	n=62	n=56	n=25	n=117	n=49	n=11

Table 9.7
Local government experience of departing MPs, by election

Election	Conservative Total MPs	Coun-cil	No. MPs	%	Labour Total MPs	Coun-cil	No. MPs	%	Other Total MPs	Coun-cil	No. MPs
1945	45	CB	2	4·4	132	CB	19	14·4	21	CB	1
		B	1	2·2		B	28	21·2		B	3
		CC	5	11·1		CC	19	14·4		CC	–
		UDC	–	–		UDC	2	1·5		UDC	1
		Total		17·7		Total		51·5			
		None	37	82·3		None	64	48·5		None	16
		Total	45	100·0		Total	132	100·0		Total	21
1950	24	CB	2	8·3	37	CB	9	24·3	4	CB	–
		B	–	–		B	4	10·8		B	–
		CC	4	16·7		CC	2	5·4		CC	–
		UDC	–	–		UDC	1	2·7		UDC	–
		Total		25·0		Total		43·2			
		None	18	75·0		None	21	56·8		None	4
		Total	24	100·0		Total	37	100·0		Total	4
1951	56	CB	2	3·6	49	CB	6	12·2	2	CB	–
		B	3	5·4		B	11	22·4		B	–
		CC	6	10·7		CC	2	4·1		CC	1
		UDC	–	–		UDC	1	2·0		UDC	–
		Total		19·7		Total		40·7			
		None	45	80·3		None	29	59·3		None	1
		Total	56	100·0		Total	49	100·0		Total	2
1955	83	CB	2	2·4	62	CB	8	12·9	4	CB	–
		B	5	6·0		B	9	14·5		B	–
		CC	6	7·2		CC	9	14·5		CC	–
		UDC	2	2·4		UDC	4	6·5		UDC	–
		Total		18·0		Total		48·4			
		None	68	82·0		None	32	51·6		None	4
		Total	83	100·0		Total	62	100·0		Total	4
1959	115	CB	15	13·1	56	CB	10	17·9	4	CB	–
		B	3	2·6		B	7	12·5		B	–
		CC	8	7·0		CC	5	8·9		CC	–
		UDC	1	0·9		UDC	5	8·9		UDC	–
		Total		23·6		Total		48·2			
		None	88	76·4		None	29	51·8		None	4
		Total	115	100·0		Total	56	100·0		Total	4
1964	54	CB	4	7·4	25	CB	3	12·0	2	CB	–
		B	5	9·3		B	3	12·0		B	–
		CC	3	5·6		CC	2	8·0		CC	–
		UDC	2	3·7		UDC	1	4·0		UDC	–
		Total		26·0		Total		36·0			
		None	40	74·0		None	16	64·0		None	2
		Total	54	100·0		Total	25	100·0		Total	2

(Table continued overleaf)

Table 9.7 (continued)

Election	Total MPs	Conservative Coun-cil	No. MPs	%	Total MPs	Labour Coun-cil	No. MPs	%	Total MPs	Other Coun-cil	No. MPs
1966	42	CB	1	2·3	117	CB	15	12·8	4	CB	–
		B	7	16·7		B	20	17·1		B	–
		CC	1	2·3		CC	5	4·3		CC	1
		UDC	1	2·3		UDC	10	8·5		UDC	–
		Total		23·6		Total		42·7			
		None	32	76·4		None	67	57·3		None	3
		Total	42	100·0		Total	117	100·0		Total	4
1970	88	CB	7	8·0	49	CB	5	10·2	2	CB	–
		B	5	5·7		B	6	12·2		B	–
		CC	5	5·7		CC	2	4·1		CC	–
		UDC	1	1·1		UDC	3	6·1		UDC	–
		Total		20·5		Total		32·6			
		None	70	79·5		None	33	67·4		None	2
		Total	88	100·0		Total	49	100·0		Total	2
Feb. 1974	33	CB	4	12·1	11	CB	2	18·2	5	CB	–
		B	3	9·1		B	–	–		B	–
		CC	3	9·1		CC	1	9·1		CC	1
		UDC	3	9·1		UDC	–	–		UDC	–
		Total		39·4		Total		27·3			
		None	20	60·6		None	8	72·7		None	4
		Total	33	100·0		Total	11	100·0		Total	5

Index